Tune-Ups

Kabbalah Publishing is a registered DBA of
The Kabbalah Centre International, Inc.

For further information:

The Kabbalah Centre
155 E. 48th St., New York, NY. 10017
1062 S. Robertson Blvd., Los Angeles, CA 90035

1.800.Kabbalah
www.kabbalah.com

First Edition
February 2009
Printed in Canada
ISBN13: 978-1-57189-619-3

Design: HL Design (Hyun Min Lee) www.hldesignco.com

100%

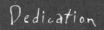

Dedication

For any and everyone seeking a better way to live;
this book is for you.

Introduction

Why This Book

For the last five years, my *Daily Tune-Ups* have been e-mailed to Kabbalah students worldwide, who look to them each morning to help start their day with their consciousness on the right track. The subscriber base has grown exponentially by word of mouth. I have gotten such positive feedback from people about how these short messages have helped them change their lives for the better that it made sense to me to collect the best of my *Tune-Ups* in a book, in order to reach a wider audience. It is my hope—and my belief—that this book will benefit anyone who is looking for a way not just to cope but to thrive in these challenging times. And for those of you who have been receiving my e-mails, this book can serve as a sort of refresher course, or simply, a more permanent record of Kabbalah's timeless wisdom.

* * * * * * *

Why You See Two Dates at the Top of Each Page

Kabbalah teaches that each day of the year affords a particular window of opportunity, and if we increase our awareness of this, we can take advantage of it to make our lives better and the world a better place. But the dates are not the same every year, as they are on the Gregorian calendar. Thus, in 2009, the first

day of the first month—*Nissan* and the sign of
Aries—falls on March 26; and in 2010, it will fall on
March 16.

* * * * * * *

The Kabbalistic Calendar Versus the Gregorian Calendar

Most of us in the western world follow the
Gregorian calendar, which is based on the Earth's
orbit around the sun and is divided into 365 days
(366 every four years). With this solar-based
calendar, the position of the sun relative to the
seasons is always the same. For example, summer
(in the northern hemisphere) always begins around
June 21. The kabbalistic calendar, however, is based
on the lunar year (i.e., the orbit of the moon around
the Earth), with 12 months of 29 or 30 days each,
and each month corresponding to one of the
12 signs of the zodiac. In order to keep kabbalistic
holiday observances within the required season of
the solar year, the lunar year must be reconciled
with the solar year, otherwise those holidays would
wander through different seasons. To maintain
this relationship between the two ways of marking
time, the kabbalistic year turns the calendar back to
zero by adding a 13th month seven times in every
19 years (always a second month of Pisces).

How To Use This Book

Simply turn to today's page; read, and contemplate. Each daily tune-up is based on the wisdom of Kabbalah and its major text, the *Zohar*, and is meant to help you get your consciousness in shape by identifying and using that day's energy to recognize the signs and messages that come to you every day.

* * * * * * *

An orange star at the top of a page marks the days on which there is extra Light available to all of us. You can increase your connection to the Light even more on these days.

March / April

The Light is ever merciful, giving us endless fresh starts and countless do-overs. Every moment is an opportunity to plant a positive seed, even when the last moment was less than positive.

This is especially so during the next 12 days. You see, today begins the new lunar year, and with it comes the power to start all over again.

The famed 16th century Kabbalist, Rav Isaac Luria (the Ari), teaches that each of the first 12 days of Aries corresponds to and directly influences each of the 12 months of the year. For example, day one of Aries corresponds to the month of Aries, day two to the month of Taurus, and so on. Why is this important to know? Because how you think and act on these 12 days affects the shape and future of the upcoming months. As Kabbalist Rav Berg states, *"Aries is the battleground to determine the outcome of all battles that will arise during the next 12 months."* This means that each of the first 12 days of Aries presents us with an opportunity to overcome whatever it is that normally blocks us from receiving the fulfillment we deserve. How we respond to the tests of the first 12 days affects the outcome of how we experience the coming year.

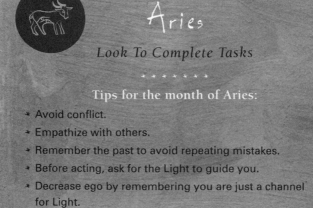

Aries

Look To Complete Tasks

* * * * * *

Tips for the month of Aries:

* Avoid conflict.
* Empathize with others.
* Remember the past to avoid repeating mistakes.
* Before acting, ask for the Light to guide you.
* Decrease ego by remembering you are just a channel for Light.

The constant self-reflection and desire to elevate that is required of spiritual work is not easy. It is not uncommon to think: "I'm fine the way I am. Why must I fix what isn't broken?"

This mind-set is actually spiritual slavery. This type of thinking leads us to stay in the wrong relationship or an unfulfilling job, simply to avoid the painful process of self-understanding and change.

Resist the temptation to be a slave today. Push yourself. Find a way to go to a new level in whatever it is you are doing.

Taurus

Avoid Being Comfortable; If It's Uncomfortable, Do It

∗ ∗ ∗ ∗ ∗ ∗ ∗

Tips for the month of Taurus:
∗ Listen to others.
∗ Embrace discomfort.
∗ Actively share with others.
∗ Avoid complacency.

7 Tune-Ups

Are you ready to patch up some holes today?

Kabbalah teaches that all negativity enters our lives because we create the openings. One way we do this is through unfulfilled vows. When we make a promise to do something, the Light gives us the energy to fulfill it. But when we don't fulfill our promise, the energy burns and creates space for depression, low self-esteem, purposelessness, and all the rest to enter.

Pull one project out from that abandoned drawer within your mind. Dust if off and take one action step today toward getting it up and running.

Gemini

Focus and Commit

✴ ✴ ✴ ✴ ✴ ✴ ✴

Tips for the month of Gemini:

* Focus on one thing at a time.
* Finish what you start.
* Trust the Light, not your rational mind.

What are you afraid of?

A recent study showed that most people spend an average of one to eight hours a day worrying. Only 8 percent of those fears actually come to fruition.

The kabbalists teach us to walk through the brick walls of our fears with certainty and trust, knowing that freedom and happiness await us on the other side.

Take a risk today. I can give you a million examples of risk-taking, but only you know when you are going out on a limb and when you are playing it safe under the covers.

Cancer

Take Risks

✳ ✳ ✳ ✳ ✳ ✳ ✳

Tips for the month of Cancer:

* Live in the NOW.
* Let go of fears.
* Realize that all the money in the world can't give you a sense of security—only connection to the Light can.
* Do a sharing action daily.
* Count your blessings.

Do people hear you when you speak?

Using our words to convey a message is only half the task of communicating. To exemplify what we say by what we do is the second half of the task. If we show what we mean through our own example, people will eventually be able to learn by example alone.

Be extra cautious and aware of your actions today. Live your life as an exclamation, not an explanation.

Leo

You Don't Have To Be Everyone's Friend

✶ ✶ ✶ ✶ ✶ ✶ ✶

Tips for the month of Leo:

* Think before speaking.
* Use strength to help others, not to dominate them.
* Be more empathetic; understand another's perspective.
* Be sensitive to another person's feelings.
* Don't be the center of attention.

Are you quick to judge?

If you want to have any chance of escaping the shortsightedness of your ego, then you'll want to refrain from slamming down the gavel of judgment too quickly.

Today, hold off on passing sentences until you've asked yourself, "Do I see the whole picture? Is there something I've missed?"

Virgo

Beware of Being Critical of Yourself (and Others)

✦ ✦ ✦ ✦ ✦ ✦

Tips for the month of Virgo:

* Seek to understand, not judge.
* Look for the good (not the bad) in everything.
* Don't be so sensitive to criticism.
* Let go of the desire to control everything.

She loves me, she loves me not.
She loves me, she loves me not.
She loves me, she loves me not.

Make up your mind, already!

So what if you put your heart on the chopping block
and the ax does fall? What's the worst that can happen?
Just remember that getting hurt helps you get to
your next level. As long as you're aware of that, no
effort is in vain and everything is great. Everything.

Don't think so much today. Just do it. And do it with
certainty, passion, and love.

Libra

Make Decisions with Certainty

＊ ＊ ＊ ＊ ＊ ＊ ＊

Tips for the month of Libra:

* Don't second-guess yourself.
* Share because you care, not because you want love.
* Don't fall prey to F.E.A.R. (False Evidence Appearing
  Real).

Am I bothering you? You wouldn't be bothered if you knew what I've been through.

Kabbalah teaches that all the good reasons we have to be mad at people vanish once we take a peek behind the curtain. And the more we ask the Light to help us understand the pain that drives a person, the more we become able to see that pain.

Resist holding on to bad feelings today. Open your heart. Focus the laser of your compassion on those who get under your skin.

Scorpio

Love Yourself More;
Be Jealous of Others Less

∗ ∗ ∗ ∗ ∗ ∗ ∗

Tips for the month of Scorpio:

* Stay calm; don't be a drama queen.
* Don't blame your distress on others.
* Channel your intense energy into helping (not hurting) others.
* Beware of your appetite for destruction and revenge.

Have you ever spoken words you wish you could take back?

Today, pay special attention to the criticism that comes out of your mouth. It's easy to tell people what you really think of them in the heat of the moment, but it's not so easy to take back those words once you cool off.

Be mindful of your mouth today. Blurting out comments can lead to many troubles, whereas thinking before you speak can bring miracles and wonders.

Sagittarius

*Stand Up for Something
You Believe In*

* * * * * * *

Tips for the month of Sagittarius:

* Practice forgiveness.
* Pay attention to the little things.
* Make a commitment and stick to it.
* Analyze the whole situation before making a decision.
* Be more sensitive to others; watch what you say.

W*hat you see is what you get*—NOT!

Unfortunately, we fixate on material proof and tangible results to justify our spiritual work. However, there is no time, space, or motion in the 99 Percent Realm, and therefore no waiting in line, no money, and no need for travel. Everything you need exists in the here and now.

In which ways are you too attached to the outcome of your efforts in life? Spend time today detaching: Focus on the process and not the end result.

Capricorn

Trust When It Isn't Easy;
Break Some of Your Rules

✦ ✦ ✦ ✦ ✦ ✦ ✦

Tips for the month of Capricorn:

* Express your emotions.
* Realize it's not the physical things you want but the Light within them.
* Appreciate what you have (it's the secret to getting more).
* Activate your enormous spiritual potential by realizing possessions are ephemeral.

15   Tune-Ups

When you argue, do you hold on to your opinions at all costs?

Sometimes we think like a boiled egg—the longer we boil, the harder we become. We cling to our own opinions, and the more people oppose us, the harder we hold on—no matter who gets hurt.

Today, soften your resolve in situations. Listen and learn from your adversaries. Master the valuable art of conceding.

Don't be an egghead.

Aquarius
Try to Conform;
Do What Someone Else Does

* * * * * * *

Tips for the month of Aquarius:

* Allow people to love you.
* Feel the suffering of the guy next to you.
* Don't be so stubborn.
* If you want to change the world, you must change yourself first.
* Yes, you are a genius. But remember, you are only a channel for this brilliance.

What is unconditional love?

Unconditional love is accepting someone as he or she is, without judgment. And it doesn't just "happen." It is a mountain we must climb, constantly fighting our fatigue, restricting our desire to give up, drawing on our compassion and inner strengths we knew nothing of, and looking to the peak even when we've been knocked down to our hands and knees. This is unconditional love.

Who needs your unconditional love today? Find a way to put your judgments aside. Love people for who they are.

Pisces

Stop Feeling Sorry for Yourself

✳ ✳ ✳ ✳ ✳ ✳ ✳

Tips for the month of Pisces:

* Be a leader.
* Initiate action.
* Balance logic and emotion.
* Handle pressure with certainty.
* Go the extra mile.
* Feel other people's pain, not your own.

Are you the same as you were a year ago?

If so, maybe it's time to shake things up a bit. What is preventing you from moving forward and from discovering new parts of yourself? Where are you still the Effect—and not the Cause—of your life?

We keep coming up against the same old issues: Doubting our power; fearing what people think of us; holding on to pain from our childhood. There comes a point in every person's life when they must realize, "I can't outrun my darkness—I can only fill it with Light."

That point is today ... and every day.

The ego is a funny thing. It convinces us that we're right. And even when we're wrong, it convinces us that we don't need to apologize, acknowledge, or reconcile. And at that moment, the ego is anything but a funny thing.

Today is the perfect day to turn around and look back, without letting your ego impair your vision. Look into your past for someone to whom you failed to show compassion, and show that compassion now. It may not even require an apology—just a little effort to close the gap between you and that person.

Maybe one day you'll both be able to look back on your funny egos and laugh.

The day after *Pesach*, we enter a 49-day period known as the Counting of the *Omer*. It's a journey inward to find and uproot the faults and weaknesses in our character. It prepares us for *Shavuot*, when we have the chance to forge a union between the Essence of God (the Light) and the physical world (the Vessel), producing total perfection.

Within our system we have parasite-like entities that the kabbalists call *klipot*. These *klipot* feed off the same thing from which our soul gains its nourishment: The Lightforce of the Creator. These *klipot* prevent a perfect union between Light and Vessel.

Every action we take feeds either our soul or our *klipot*.

Over the next seven weeks we have the opportunity to break open the husks of these parasites from within our being, releasing the Light that has been trapped by our own choices. Yes, the extraction process may be painful. But the benefits of releasing the trapped sparks of Light are more than worth it.

Today, recall any nasty habits or unpleasant character traits that you cannot get rid of. The energy of the day will help you find the discipline you need to triumph over all self-centered impulses and negative desires.

It is written in the Torah, "and He called," referring to God's calling to Moses. Many times you are called by God. He gives you messages all the time, in dreams and through other people, but you don't always hear them.

In order to hear, you need to make your ego small. In order to make your ego small, you must be open to everything. Being open to every single thing that happens in your life—whether it is positive or negative—means knowing the Light brings it to your doorstep for a reason.

When you open yourself to the endless possibilities of the Light, you are that much closer to hearing God.

My mom, Karen Berg, has this amazing concept she uses in her lectures that she calls "*erase yourself*." It means taking yourself out of the picture, especially when you cast a judgmental eye on others.

Practice erasing yourself all day today. This doesn't mean becoming a doormat. It means removing your agendas, biases, preconceived notions, and grudges. Simply put: Erase yourself.

You may have read the biblical story of Moses's encounter with the burning bush. One day while wandering in the desert, he hears God calling to him from a burning bush, telling him to free the Israelites from Egyptian slavery. The rest is history. Here's an interesting fact: The kabbalists say that, initially, Moses did not hear God's voice. Moses actually heard the voice of his own father calling him. Why? He needed to hear a voice that was friendly and familiar in order to draw him closer. He would have been too afraid if he knew who was really calling.

Just as God understood what Moses needed to hear (and the voice he needed to hear it in), God knows what we need. Our Creator meets us where we are on our journey, making sure that the events and people in our lives are tailor-made for our spiritual growth.

Remember this today when you are wondering why you must go through one difficult situation or another.

One of the best pieces of advice I received before getting married was this: Apologize when you're wrong, and apologize when she's wrong!

When we love someone, it doesn't matter if we are right. So what? The whole purpose of relationships is oneness. There's no oneness when you are sitting on your side of the bed, calculating and figuring out what you did right and what she did wrong. And this goes for relationships of all stripes—with our parents, our friends, or our kids.

Today, swallow your pride and apologize to someone with whom you've been at odds.

Egypt in Hebrew is *Mitzrayim*, which comes from the word *tzar* (narrow). It's a code for our tendency to stick with whatever chaos we're dealing with simply because it's what we know. We stay with low self-esteem, which leads to bad habits, which leads to limited opportunities.

What *mitzrayim* do you need to rise up out of? Every time you find yourself in the same outcome, think of a new and proactive way to handle the situation. If you want new outcomes in your life, you have to deal with your challenges differently. You have to open your mind to different ways of seeing. The same solutions for the same problems lead to the same outcomes.

Do you realize that when you are in a fit of anger, it's synonymous with saying there is no God?

Think about it. The Light is constantly feeding you growth opportunities—the more uncomfortable, the more potential for growth. When you're losing it, overpowered by feelings of rage, you're basically admitting that God has left the building.

Knowing that the Light sent this situation to you is a matter of consciousness. However, when you're sitting in bumper-to-bumper summer traffic with a broken A/C, late for a job interview, and some guy just blocked you from making your exit, it's not so easy to be Mr. or Mrs. Spiritual, is it?

When you find yourself unleashing your middle finger and searching for the choicest curse words, try repeating to yourself over and over: "What is the Light teaching ME?"

I don't expect you to achieve this state of consciousness today. It takes repetition. But the more awareness you inject, the easier it gets to pull yourself out of the fire of your own feelings.

If we want to grow spiritually, then we must resign ourselves to the fact that cleansing the ego hurts. If we are afraid of feeling pain, then we are afraid of growing.

Let's say you are completely humiliated by someone. Instead of letting the insult simmer for days, weeks, or years, you can surrender to the bruising and focus on the bigger goal of transformation and purification. You can allow yourselves to feel the pain of humiliation, and you can move on faster by saying, "Great! Just what I need—a good ego-bashing to help me change and purify!"

Forget about feeling good 100 percent of the time. If we are not going through some downs, then we can't have those ups we love so much. Today, see everything in terms of the big picture of your spiritual journey. And release the need for immediate gratification in every moment.

We can make a $2 donation to a charity, or pass out flyers for a grassroots organization, and be discouraged by the thought, "This is just a small donation. I am just one person. My contributions don't mean very much." Or, we can focus on the big picture and realize how important every positive action of sharing is to the quantum collective consciousness.

Rav Ashlag wrote:

> When a person is weighing sesame seeds, he continues adding one at a time until the weighing is completed. Every seed does its share in the weighing, for without it, the process would not be completed.

Today, remember that through our consistent positive actions, we all have the power to affect global change and to remove chaos from the world.

Rav Isaac Luria (the Ari) teaches us that we are each responsible for 2000 souls. We do not see it, but there are invisible cords tying us to other people we've never met. Every time we have a personal breakthrough, 2000 other people have a breakthrough. Every time we lose a personal battle….You get the picture.

If our goal is to remove only the chaos from our own lives, then we are limited in how effective we can be. Every goal is a Vessel; the bigger the goal, the bigger the Vessel and, therefore, the greater the Vessel's capacity for Light.

This doesn't mean that we shouldn't be interested in Light for ourselves. But without thinking and focusing on the bigger picture, we limit the amount of Light we can receive.

Today, realize that every time you believe in yourself despite your doubt; every time you act with tolerance despite feeling intolerant; every time you share when you'd rather receive, you are making it easier for 2000 other people to do so as well. Always think of the bigger goal: The removal of chaos from other people's lives.

I know a lot of people who are what you'd call hard-core Kabbalah students: Attending holidays, studying the *Zohar*, doing acts of charity, reading the books, etc. Yet they're not really changing. And they ask me, "Why am I still in this dysfunctional relationship, or dealing with low self-esteem, or battling this addiction? Why am I not changing?"

I tell them what my father and teacher, the Rav, has often told me, *"Change is what happens when the pain of staying the same is greater than the pain of changing."*

The thing is, we don't want to wait for the pain of cancer to motivate us to stop smoking, or the heartbreak of a lover cheating on us to realize we're in a bad relationship. We want to imagine what the pain would feel like now, so we don't have to go through it later.

What do you want to change about yourself? Pick one thing and imagine the pain you will feel down the line if you continue doing what you are doing. And then change it.

Most of us dread commitment and assignments. We prefer to do what we want, when we want, and don't you dare tell me what to do. But the kabbalists explain that dedication and commitment, while imprisoning for the body, are truly freeing for the soul.

This time of year, more than ever, it's important to create a structure or regimen, not just for your spiritual advancement but for your physical progress as well.

With that in mind, what can you commit to today that will help set your soul free?

Today (as almost every day), you will feel compelled to judge and criticize others. But before you do, ask yourself, "Would I be as quick to get this person a cup of coffee?"

If the answer is yes, then let 'er rip—with two spoons of compassion, of course. But if you'd hold back on the coffee, then hold back on the criticism as well.

You'll get your own cup of love from the universe in return.

Sometimes, the greatest sacrifice we can make is not being right. You know how it is when you get into it with a friend, or spouse, or colleague, and they just don't get it. What's wrong with them?! How many relationships have we left in our wake because we couldn't let go of being right?

My father and teacher, the Rav, always told me that the cemetery is filled with people who are right. Meaning, how important is it if you have to give a little, to sacrifice your pride? What's more important, being right and alone, or wrong and with the Light?

Today, don't be afraid to say, "Fine, you're right." It's OK; it won't kill you. Your ego may take a beating, but you'll get over it. And you'll be better off for it.

The great Rav Chaim Vital (student of Rav Isaac Luria, the Ari) wrote this on the subject of anger:

Take the anger and sadness out of your heart because these traits will be obstacles between you and the Light. Make every effort to love the people around you and be happy even when not everything goes as you want.

Great advice, except he himself was well-known for his anger problems. The Ari often took him to a special lake where he immersed his student in waters that were said to remove rage. The point is, we all need to hear this advice, but this isn't to say we are bad if we do get angry. As long as we are conscious of what we're trying to achieve, and working at it, then we're on the right path.

Today, work on taking the anger and sadness out of your heart. Forgive those people you find so annoying. Maybe even give them some love? I'm sure they can use it; that's probably why they are being so annoying in the first place.

April / May

I don't know about you, but for me, this *Omer* (the 49 days between *Passover* and *Shavuot*) is starting to get hairy. Every day a different piece of my personal garbage floats to the surface. It feels like that scene in *Star Wars* when Luke and his companions get trapped in the garbage disposal and the walls start closing in on them.

But I wouldn't want it any other way. The *Omer* is concentrated soul-correction time. Whereas the rest of the year I have to search for what needs fixing, the *Omer* shoves it right in my face. Whatever my issues are, the Light sends me the people and situations that push my buttons, giving me the motivation to eliminate these buttons altogether.

The bottom line during this time of year is to be thankful for the pressure, because it forces us to deal with our garbage. I know, it's easier said than done. That's why I've been studying the *Zohar* more, and making sure that I am positioning myself in service to others as much as possible. The combination of help from above and helping myself are giving me the clarity and the courage to embrace the discomfort and actually sort of enjoy it. Emphasis on "sort of."

Complacency. Anyone on a spiritual path faces it sooner or later. It's when you think, "I've got the hang of this restriction thing," or worse, "Wow, I'm really changing." It's the perception that the work you're doing is enough to keep you protected, safe, and enlightened. But as long as you are alive, there is always more to be revealed. Enough is never enough. If you're overly satisfied with yourself, it's a sure sign you need to change something.

Which spiritual practices have you let fall by the wayside? Choose one and recommit to it today, with all your heart and passion.

Tremendous opportunities for growth await us when we are less consumed with our own pain and more concerned with the pain of others. When we see other people going through difficult times, we need to feel their pain as if it were our own.

This might sound simple and familiar, but it is neither.

The sages explain to us that the reason to feel another's pain is not to be deemed good or spiritual; paradoxically, it should be done for selfish reasons. Every time we put ourselves in someone else's shoes, the effort we make at feeling their pain removes an illusory curtain that separates us from them. This process mirrors our connection with the Light—the closer we come to feeling the people around us, the closer we can get to the Light.

Pick at least one person today and feel their pain. If you can't feel their pain, study a section of the *Zohar*, and ask its author, Rav Shimon bar Yochai, to open your heart.

How are you?

One of life's most frequently asked questions—and least answered.

Examine how present you are in your relationships today. Are you taking the time to care about the people with whom you are speaking, or are you rushing off to your next priority?

Slow it up today. Offer signs of love and caring to people. Be the compassionate, caring person you want others to be.

What actions of sharing did you take today?

If fire does not burn brightly, tap the wood, and it blazes forth. If the Light of the soul does not burn brightly, tap the body, so that the Light of the soul should blaze forth.
—The *Zohar*

It's all about action. If we hope to achieve any level of real contentment in life, then we must "tap the body," do what's uncomfortable, and go against the gravity of our physical urges. Commit to spending time this week doing some form of volunteering. Acts of sharing will set your soul free.

I can't talk now, too busy.

It's so easy to be "busy" in life, to get caught up in the details of staying alive: Paying the rent, working out, fixing the leaks, or finding shoes that fit. Sure, it's all important. But is it more important than the people we love? How often do we overlook the needs of those closest to us because we just can't seem to fit them into our schedule?

Make yourself available today. When you look back at your life, it's not what you did that you'll remember, but who you did it with.

Peace of mind comes when your body is in constant motion.

The great early 20th century Kabbalist, Rav Ashlag, would stand long hours on his feet until, in his later years, he began to suffer chronic ailments. Rav Ashlag said to his students:

> *"If it seems that in a sitting situation the mind is more at ease and settled, it is not so; rather, the more you tire and toil the body, the deliberations in the brain come to brighter clarity."*

The word for today is *effort*. See how hard you can push yourself. If you are the type to go the extra mile, then go the extra-extra mile.

These are tough days. I see the pain and frustration everywhere I go. I, myself, am struggling with the right words, the right thoughts. As often as I can, I remind myself of Rav Shimon's words:

> Wisdom is *actually revealed by way of its opposite, folly. Just as Light would not be known without darkness, or white without black, nor sweet without bitter, or health without illness, God has made the one as well as the other.*
> —The *Zohar*

With every pain and fear and doubt I experience, I remind myself that as bad as it gets, that's how great my joy and my certainty and my peace will be when I pass these tests the *Omer* is presenting to me.

Not a day goes by that I don't get hit on the head (metaphorically speaking).

If it's not a reader telling me what's wrong with my grammar, logic, thoughts, or attitude, then it's a blogger sloughing me off or a media person telling the world what I am doing wrong. You know what? I love it. Not at first, but over time I've learned to love the criticism. It's good for my soul; it shows me where I need to improve, and it keeps me humble.

It's like weight lifting: Nevermind the sore muscles, just keep on lifting.

Today, let in the unpleasant feedback. If you really want to be brave, then go on the offensive and ask friends and strangers, "What do I need to improve?"

We all have our garbage and we each suffer as a result of not cleaning it up. But we are not the only ones. The stink travels.

Today, be aware that the negativity within you has affected other people besides yourself. Bring someone to whom you have caused pain into your awareness today. Feel the distress you have caused them. Then imagine this person forgiving you. And after really feeling the pain you caused, forgive yourself as well.

What do we do with those people who push our buttons? Going off on someone verbally only hurts us. But suppressing those feelings robs us of as much energy as expressing it verbally.

What is to be done?!

Sometimes, it's vital to get just a little distance from the button-pushers in order to set our mind in a better direction. Today, if you find yourself lit up, take a walk; get a change of scenery. Do anything that will change up your energy.

Try it, and you will see amazing results.

Argggggggggggggggggggggggggh!

Do you ever feel that rage? More appropriately, how many minutes has it been since you did? There are many explanations for the spiritual and emotional triggers of anger, and many tips on how to defuse them. But once we are in the throes of anger, neat and tidy explanations don't help us much.

Three days. That's the amount of time kabbalists recommend waiting before confronting the object of your frustration. Sure, your kids/coworkers/subordinates/mother-in-law/accountant/Little League coach/hairdresser/grandfather/gardener/ex-wife/future wife need a wake-up call, and you're the one to give it to them.

But not until you cool down. Otherwise, they won't hear a word you're saying.

When someone comes to you with a problem, what's your first reaction? Do you try to fix it or feel it?

The compulsion to fix people comes from our own feelings of inadequacy. Because others mirror our own garbage (and no one likes to see their own junk), we scramble to cover it up with platitudes: "You'll be fine;" "Trust the Light;" "Go share."

But think about the people in your life who help you the most. Is it their words or their love that set you straight when you're getting off track? A little of both. If you want to do the same for another person, you've got to turn down the rhetoric and turn up the love.

Recently, I met a man who lives out on a ranch and hasn't any interest in spirituality and God and all that. But he's been through his fair share of tests, ordeals that would have sent most of us packing. I asked him how he does it, how he keeps fighting those seemingly insurmountable battles—and winning.

He told me, "It's simple: When bad things happen, you make them good. And when you do that long enough, you reach a state where you realize only good things happen."

Today, forget about looking for the silver lining, and searching for why this is happening, and faking it 'til you make it. Put all that on hold for today. Instead, jump right into that awareness—only good things happen.

It's important to be tolerant with yourself—especially during the *Omer*. If you can't love yourself, who can you love? Really, how are you supposed to see the truth in your relationships if your relationship with yourself is totally upside down?

What does it really mean to love yourself? It means you love the Creator within you. It means you appreciate that there is a spark of the Lightforce of the Creator that exists within you; it's that part of you that can channel the right words and help someone truly transform a negative situation. This part of you is indeed very lovable, because it is an emanation of the Light. When kabbalists speak about loving yourself, it is this part that they're talking about.

This is the part of yourself you want to make every effort to connect to today, as often as possible.

You can take a rock from the river that has been there for two days and a rock that has been there for two years, lay them on the riverbank, and they will both dry at the same time.

It doesn't matter how long you've been holding on to your garbage. The moment you reach the point where you don't want it anymore is the moment you release it, and the healing begins.

Push yourself today and really look at those parts of yourself that you've been avoiding. Go up to one person today and ask them to tell you one thing you need to fix. It will hurt—if it's true—but it will also liberate you from feeling the need to hide from what you need to do.

Have you heard about the man who begged God for years to allow him to win the lottery? Every day, he got down on his knees and shouted to Heaven, "Please let today be the day I win!" After a year of no response, he went to his teacher to ask what he was doing wrong. His teacher asked him, "Did you buy a ticket?"

It's a great place to be when you recognize the existence of the Creator and learn how to humbly ask for help. But the secret to getting your prayers answered is this:

> *"God translates our prayers based on our actions."*
> — Karen Berg

Today, perform an act of random kindness (especially for someone you don't like). Resist the temptation to judge people. Go out of your way to help a co-worker. Cross the street to help a stranded stranger. Listen closely to someone you normally drown out. Open up someone who's being difficult by using gratitude. Every positive action, every restriction, every conscious effort to emulate the attributes of the Light will ensure that your prayers are heard, loud and clear.

What was the magic ingredient that allowed Rav Shimon Bar Yochai to reveal the secrets of the universe contained in the *Zohar*? Genius? Wisdom? Ambition?

The answer is unity. It was the love between Rav Shimon Bar Yochai's students that opened the Divine Gates, inviting the wisdom of the Light to come through. Specifically, they loved each other's garbage! As we know, it's easy to love when people do our bidding, but not so easy when they rub us the wrong way.

If we're going to have a shot at spinning this Earth on a different axis, then we've got to put in great effort toward extending compassion and human dignity to everyone. Today, focus on one person you cannot stand and see what you can do about melting the ice around your heart.

For those of us who want to change the world, it's essential to remember that when we make small changes in ourselves, we reveal the spark of God within. This is what creates change in the world.

Small changes are by no means easy, as you know. Over time, we create negative habits, which we unconsciously follow. Stopping these habits is like holding back a tidal wave. But it's not totally impossible. We can do it. It just takes a lot of our effort. Scratch that, it takes ALL our effort, but we can do it. And when we do overcome ourselves, we allow the Light of our souls to illuminate the people in our immediate circle and beyond.

Bottom line: Today, when you face a challenge, refuse to react in your usual way. Choose a new direction; be proactive. This is not only how you will change your life, but it's how you will change the world. You can do it.

Pessimists are usually right and optimists are usually wrong, but most great changes were made by optimists. I read that somewhere and it resonates with me and with a lot of us here at The Kabbalah Centre, where our mission is nothing less than the removal of death from the lexicon of the universal vocabulary.

Not an easy task; not even a logical task, but it's a task to which myself and thousands around the world have dedicated their lives. And we're doing it with the technology of Kabbalah (or as my father, the Rav, calls it: 25th century science) and the technology of converting the ego's desires into the soul's desires.

It's through small personal changes that our goal will be accomplished. Keep looking for ways in which you can change reflexive behavior into proactive behavior, hatred into unconditional love, and intolerance into compassion. Let's prove those pessimists wrong, once and for all.

Molasses. These days, I'm covered in it. At least that's what it feels like trudging through the *Omer*, people yelling at me left and right. I can really feel the negativity weighing people down.

That's why I'm taking it easy and avoiding conflict, even with myself. Just lots of deep breaths and a commitment to stop fighting every thought, and letting the Light do some of the heavy lifting. When I stop fighting the Universe the Universe stops fighting me.

Let go today. OK, so that lady totally cut in front of you and took the last banana walnut bran muffin, the one you had your eyes on. Let her have it. OK, so you're going crazy trying to find a job and there's nothing out there. Keep plugging away and something will open up. OK, your husband is pushing buttons you didn't even know existed. Give him some space. Take a night out with the girls. Let it go.

This is only a test. Let go, and you'll pass with flying colors.

There once was a woman whose young son was diabetic and couldn't stop eating sweets. The mother decided to seek out Mahatma Gandhi's wisdom. She and her son rode a train for three days to seek the advice of the renowned spiritual leader.

When they arrived at his home, they waited in line for hours, until they were finally invited to speak with him. Once the mother explained the story, Gandhi replied, "Please come back in thirty days." Rather than travel back and forth, the woman and her son found temporary housing, and she took a job as a dishwasher at a local restaurant.

After thirty days, they returned to Gandhi, seeking his advice yet again. This time, Gandhi stood up, held the boy by his shoulders, and said, "My son, you must stop eating sugar." The mother was enraged. "With all due respect, we traveled a great distance to seek your counsel, and this is all you have to tell us?" Gandhi replied, "Madam, I could not ask your son to do something that I myself could not do. Only yesterday was I able to completely cut sugar out of my diet."

Today's lesson is plain: We cannot expect others to do things we aren't able to do ourselves!

"You should judge your friend justly," it is written. Initially, this sounds like a spiritual lesson most of us have heard before. In reality, there is a very important, self-centered reason why we need to judge others justly.

A long time ago, in the Holy Temple, there was a mirror in which the spirituality of a person could be seen. Today, because the Temple doesn't exist, every person is a mirror for others. What you see in other people is really within you. When you judge something you don't like in another, you're basically pointing out your own bad points.

Today, every time a judgment enters your mind, ask yourself, "What is the Light showing me about myself now?" Asking the question will lead you to your answer. Once you have seen your own flaws, you'll immediately feel more compassion toward the other person—and yourself.

Someone close to you is acting like a real jerk and you want to punch them. But you are a "spiritual" person, so you sit back and say, "Cause and Effect—the Light will take care of him."

When we wish revenge on someone, or even when we're content because we know they'll get theirs in the end, we are acting as channels of judgment. And just as a cold cup containing red-hot coffee becomes scalding, we, too, take on the very energy of judgment we wish upon others. No matter how perfect we think we are in comparison to that person, trust me, we've get our own negative files we'd rather not have the Light review.

That's why we always want to be on the side of mercy and help contribute to the solution, not the problem.

Today, focus on your ex-husband, your ex-employer, your ex-friend, or anyone you've been waiting for the Light to pounce on, and ask the Light to show them mercy. Believe me, you need it.

"Love or Need" has always been one of our most popular classes at The Kabbalah Centre. I think it's because many of us struggle with codependency and we're desperate for solutions on how to break this pattern. Needing someone else to make us feel whole is the worst feeling.

My mother and teacher, Karen Berg, writes:

> In a healthy relationship, you and your partner are interdependent. You are like the sun and the moon. The moon does not need the sun to rise, and the sun doesn't need the moon to set, but they do need each other to make the action happen in the universe.

You will have stronger, longer-lasting relationships if you are self-sufficient in this way. Today, focus on giving yourself the love and approval you so crave from others.

You will find that your journey through life with your current or future partner will be so much more beautiful for it.

After we get the basics down in our first few Kabbalah courses, we tend to stop studying. This is a huge mistake because studying is the key to expanding our spiritual potential and ingraining the truth in our minds and bodies. This is what our souls strive to do, and it is the guiding intention behind my books, and weekly and daily messages.

The great Kabbalist, Rav Moshe Chaim Luzzatto, said it best in the introduction to his classic book, *Path of the Just*:

> *I do not pretend to tell you more than you already know. But it is not what you know that shapes your life but how you know it. And in teaching you how to know, how to weave the truth of Kabbalah into the fabric of your minds and souls, to make of them heart of your heart and flesh of your flesh, is my goal to write more than a how-to book or a moral lesson and have these teachings become part of your life.*

> *Through review and persistent study you are reminded of those things which, by nature, you are prone to forget and through which you are caused to take to heart the duty and ways of being that you tend to overlook.*

One of the major problems in the world is we sometimes get so carried away in our own spiritual systems that we forget that other people have their own set of laws, too.

We get caught up in the routine part of our practice and forget the heart part.

If we want to save this world—and it certainly needs saving—then we must constantly be directing our thoughts towards compassion and tolerance for others. Only when you and I and all of us doing the work learn this lesson (and live it in our daily lives) will this world begin to spin in a different direction.

Be tolerant today. Allow others to have their opinions, no matter how wrong they may seem. Release the need to change people, to sway them to your way of thinking. Focus on love—it always does the trick.

In other words, when in doubt, hug it out.

Let's say you are someone who goes to the gym. You start out lifting five-pound weights and you can barely get them above your head. You work at it, you lose a little fat, and soon you're starting to feel great as you pump that dumbbell. A few weeks go by, and now you're not getting the same rush you had at the beginning.

It's time to pick up a bigger weight.

If you are reading this book, then you are someone who is constantly trying to create a better version of yourself. But is it possible that the five-pound weight you've been lifting the last couple of months isn't challenging you any more? Perhaps you have been doing the same sharing, or have even stopped altogether. If that's the case, than you are probably also not feeling the same excitement you had when you first starting pursuing the kabbalistic path.

In Kabbalah, you need to be constantly upgrading your life.

Today, challenge yourself to change how, why, and when you share. Share in situations that are unfamiliar, with people you have never met. Add some more weight to that barbell. Sweat a little. Get pumped!

"How do I tell the difference between restriction and repression?"

Repression is a defense mechanism that prevents unacceptable impulses from reaching consciousness. It involves some form of subconscious forgetfulness. In other words, we are not even aware we are holding down the emotions or thoughts.

When we restrict, we allow our feelings to bubble to the surface, but we make a conscious decision to hold the feeling or thought. The effort we make, over and over, eventually gives us the ability not merely to hold the reaction but to dissipate it, to melt it, to destroy it, to transform it.

Today, pay attention to how restriction and repression show up in your life. Practice makes perfect.

May / June

A chicken and a cow are walking along a crowded city street. They pass a coffee shop window where a man is sitting contentedly, eating a delicious breakfast of steak and eggs. The chicken turns to the cow and says, "That right there sums up our contribution to society."

The cow looks at him and replies, "For you, it's a contribution; for me, it's a commitment!"

This metaphor applies to our relationships with others. When we're fully connecting with our lovers, our friends, and our children, we're opening a channel for our Light to shine. But the channel only opens when we love and give 100 percent.

If you're having trouble with this, now is the time to ask for help. What is it that's blocking you? How can you get past it? You can start by choosing someone you love today and strengthening your connection to them through an act of unconditional love.

In times of pressure and stress, we usually see what someone is made of, right? That's when a person's real temperament is revealed.

Now imagine being totally stressed out. Visualize yourself being pressured by an outside source: You've got a deadline coming up, or your boyfriend is telling you that everything you do is wrong. Watch the dialogue in your head. Are you listening to the voice of the Light ("This is happening for a positive reason.") ... or are you listening to the voice of the Opponent ("Life sucks.")?

If your buttons are being triggered and you are coming from a place of hopelessness, you're listening to the Opponent.

Today is your chance to break the pattern. What could you do differently when responding to this trigger?

I hate you.

How many times during the day does that thought pop into your mind? How many times does it spill out of your mouth? How many?

If I tell you it's not nice to hate, will you stop? I don't think so. If I tell you hatred brings chaos into your life, now will you change?

> *"Turmoil is a sign of hatred."*
> —Rav Nachman of Breslov

Every time you hate someone, you are inviting a little more chaos into your life.

With that in mind, I have only one guiding question for you today. Where's the love?

Are you consistent with everyone? Do you share with the same passion with the people you dislike as you do with those whom you love?

If you want to stay connected to the Tree of Life, then you must be concerned with the energy of sharing—period. As my father and teacher, the Rav, teaches me, *"A candle lights its surroundings in the same way regardless of whether it is surrounded by light or by darkness. We must behave in the same manner, spreading Light regardless of the behavior of those around us."*

An exercise for today is to look for people you have no desire to share with: Someone you are angry with, or don't like, or don't respect, or ... you name it. Go against the urge to walk away from them and, instead, summon up something they need in the moment and give it to them—be it understanding, a smile, an apology, and so on. But don't just go through the motions—really feel it inside. That's the only way it will be real, and that's when you're channeling the energy of the Light.

Not a day or week goes by when I don't get criticized. And unlike most of us, my critiques are aired out in front of many people.

What can I say, I asked for it. The *Zohar* says we attract the people and situations that will help us grow the most. I'm not saying it feels good, but on the whole, I know no matter how cruel and cutting the comments are, this person wouldn't be saying them if there wasn't something for me to learn.

If I didn't live this principle, I would have shut down a long time ago. In fact, if my parents didn't live this principle, I wouldn't even be here to share and learn with you. In fact, if Rav Brandwein didn't live this principle, my parents wouldn't even be together to share and learn with you. In fact … you get the point.

Stay open for business today. Don't close your doors when the critics come knocking. Just the opposite: Let them in, hear them out, and learn from them. In your heart, thank them, because we learn the most from our harshest critics.

After the 49 days of the *Omer*, after having purified ourselves of the garbage we've accrued, the holiday of *Shavuot* is finally here. We have earned the Light of Freedom granted on *Pesach* and are now ready to reconnect with the Creator's Essence and receive the Light of Immortality.

Take a moment today and tonight to focus on your soul, and love yourself for the simple fact that a spark of the wonderful Creator resides within you.

> *"As the breath of the potter, so is the shape of the Vessel."*
> —The *Zohar*

Did you see *Evan Almighty*? Cute movie. The basic message was we can change the world with small acts of random kindness. I couldn't think of a more kabbalistic message.

Rav Ashlag, founder of The Kabbalah Centre in 1922, gave a simple analogy to explain this:

> *Place on one side of a balance scale sesame seeds that represent chaos, darkness, pain, and suffering, and on the other side place sesame seeds that represent unlimited fulfillment, joy, happiness, and the removal of all pain and suffering.*

Rav Ashlag then asked the question: *"How many seeds would it take to tip the scale one way or the other?"* The answer is one. And that's how we change the world. That seed could be one action of caring—one person deciding to make a difference. Too often we believe who we are isn't enough, our gestures of kindness and love won't make a difference; our ability to restrict our ego won't mean a thing in the grand scale of things. Yet, according to the kabbalists, just one action can mean the difference between darkness and Light.

Today, think about what that one sesame seed would be for you. What could tip the scales in your own life from garbage to gift, from darkness to Light, from selfishness to unconditional giving?

During the *Omer*, our ego conflicts come up nice and easily. There's no searching for what to fix. It's just there.

Now that it's over, things seem free and easy. This doesn't mean we can relax.

Today, make a list of all the issues that came up during the *Omer*. It's helpful to open a calendar and look back to see where you were emotionally during those days. Remember what was difficult for you and make sure you are still working on it even though the *Omer* is over.

Humanity is addicted to pleasure—and that's not a bad thing. Kabbalistically, pleasure is the only true reality. Love and goodness and joy—these are the attributes of the Light. The rest is illusory.

Problem is, before coming down to the physical reality, our souls struck a deal with the Creator: Let us earn our pleasure. So the Creator sends us painful situations and people that allow us to work for it. But most of us can't stand the pain, so we run toward pleasure—the temporary kind.

Today, when you are on line at Starbucks waiting for your nonfat latte with extra foam, or sneaking a cigarette, or surfing the Internet while work awaits, check in with yourself. Why are you doing this action? Is there something uncomfortable you are avoiding?

Don't get out of line, or stub out your cigarette; I'm not intending for this message to guilt-trip you. Just pay attention to what you are doing. And learn from it. Always learn from it.

A common issue for those of us studying Kabbalah is learning how to restrict properly. Often we feel guilty when a reaction bubbles to the surface, so we stuff it down. We have an issue with a friend, but we tell ourselves, "I'd better restrict." But what we really do is suppress. The anger or frustration or sadness doesn't go away—it just gets temporarily filed away.

We build up stacks of files on others, but we never bother to delete them. Eventually, the files corrupt our relationships with those whom we love.

The energy this week supports us in cleaning house. We do this by being honest with the people we care about. It is our job to educate our friends and family about how their actions affect us. Doing so relieves us of our shame, or guilt, or whatever it is we are feeling, and it helps the person on the other end understand how they are behaving and where they need to grow.

I often hear students talking about people in their lives as "not spiritual." I have to say, I never really understand what this means. I guess it's because my mother, Karen Berg, always taught me, *"If they've got a spirit, they're spiritual."* She sees everyone as a spark of the Creator.

Sure, I don't look like you and you don't look like me. That's because we are each created in the image of God differently. And for very good reason: We all have our own unique challenges to tackle in this world. Who am I to judge you as "not spiritual?"

Instead of judging people for being different than you, encourage and love them for who they are and what they do. Support them in their life process, whatever that may be.

Today, respect that everyone in your life is on their own journey. If the Light saw fit to create them and breathe life into their lungs, who are you to heap them into the unredeemable category of "not spiritual?"

Let's say you're planning a party to impress your boss. After all the plans are made, you take a trip to the plant nursery and find the finest fresh-cut orchids. The clerk wraps them up in newspaper for you and when you get home, you arrange them in your prettiest vase. You place the arrangement in the perfect setting that will draw attention and highlight the beauty of the flowers. Naturally, recognizing the beauty of the flowers often depends on the vase (which is why you don't put them in a Pringles can). You do something to accentuate it.

That is what your friends and family do for you. They help you express yourself best and fulfill your potential and destiny. It's crucial to your growth as a person that you're mindful of who you surround yourself with. The right people will bring you up; the wrong people will bring you crashing down. And it's not about whether people are inherently good or bad but about whether they are good or bad for you.

Today, think about those closest to you and ask yourself which ones bring out your best ... and which ones are just old Pringles cans.

Why is it that someone can do ten things that amount to love and ten things that amount to negativity, and we write that person off as bad? Why not focus on the good?

That is our nature. We like to fall into the darkness. And there are certainly going to be people in your life who do negative things and truly aren't meant to be in your life. But that is not who I am talking about. I am talking about people whom you truly love.

Today, focus on the positive things people do for you, and learn to compartmentalize your feelings. Meaning, don't let the tiny upsets overrule the way that you love that person. There's always going to be something that bugs you. The choice is whether or not you are willing to be there with the love, unconditionally.

Are you?

Love your neighbor as yourself. Think about what the world would look like if more of us really embraced this principle.

If every one of us devoted ourselves to totally taking care of others' needs, we'd each have billions of people looking out for us. Wouldn't be much to worry about then, would there?

Sure, sure, this is Pollyanna thinking. Or is it? Practice it today. Allow yourself a minute or an hour where you only think of ways to care for the people around you. Act on these thoughts.

What brings you joy? What really brings you that feeling of fulfillment, that sense of "This is how life was meant to be?"

Take a moment to be still. No cell phone, no computer. Put the kids to bed. Close your eyes and ask yourself, "What makes me joyful?"

Move toward that joy today. Let it color your every thought and action. When you lose focus, bring it back to the joy.

When you are in the throes of panic, it's not so easy to remember the silver lining in the dark cloud lingering over your head. But something that helps is remembering the good.

When it comes to miracles, we seem to have a short memory—out of sight, out of mind. But a powerful kabbalistic concept tells us that the more we recall the moments when the Light saved our behinds, the more certainty we will have that the Light will save us again.

Today, make a list of those miraculous moments to keep on hand in case of emergency. You might not need to refer to the list today, but it's good to have a miracle list on hand to remind you where that silver lining really is.

I've got a friend who is a real tough guy. At least that's what he wants you to think. He is terrified that you'll get a peek behind the curtain and discover how ruled he is by fear and uncertainty.

But if there is one thing I've learned from the kabbalists, it's that exposing our frailties and being vulnerable is the spiritual way. The humility it takes to reveal the truth brings us closer to the Light. That is where we find our true strength.

So, my friend, my advice to you is, come out of hiding today. Allow you to be you. What's the worst that can happen?

Still keepin' up with the Joneses? How's that working out for you?

Science tells us that out of six billion-plus people on this planet, no two people share the same DNA. And so it is with our spiritual DNA. Everyone's spark of soul is completely unique, and what works for one person might not work for another.

As my brother, Michael, says,

"The only person you need to measure yourself up against is the person you have the potential to become."

Where are you today on the road of your own transformation?

Imagine if a poor man were to marry a princess. No matter what material gifts he offered her, he would never please her because she's already had the best of everything.

And so it is with our soul.

Our soul comes from a place beyond any fulfillment we can imagine. It doesn't need flattery, respect, or validation. It has a greater purpose.

What do you think that purpose is? Talk to your soul today. Ask it what it wants from you.

Would you like to learn the secret of unconditional love?

I love you (when I don't want to).

I love you (instead of judging you).

I love you (without an agenda).

Open up today. Let people in. Show them how much love you can give.

Can your shadow move if you stand still?

Just as our shadow can't do more than we ourselves do, so too, the Light can't do for us more than we do for others.

Today, be open with others and hear what they have to say. You don't have to agree with everything, just listen. If you do, then you'll find more of your own prayers answered.

Is it hard to keep a secret when you're working on a new project?

Generally speaking, it's better to do the work first and talk about it afterwards. Kabbalists throughout history often performed their charity below the radar, out of the spotlight. They knew that blessings only rest on something that is covered from the eye.

Stay focused on your projects today—but keep it on the down-low.

Once we hear something bad about someone, it's difficult to focus on the good anymore. We start collecting evidence of bad from then on.

Why do we love to say bad things about people? Why is it so pleasurable? And why is it equally painful when we hear what people say about us?

Rather than talking about someone else today, spend time thinking about them, sending positive thoughts. And starting tomorrow, each time you are tempted to talk, just think.

Don't think. Just do.

It is said that prophesy comes from kids and fools. Why? Because they channel pure, raw information that comes from beyond the brain.

Think about a time of imminent danger, such as a near car accident, when you made that instinctual right or left that saved you from disaster. Did you have to think about it? No. You just acted. The Light guided you.

It's the thinking and analyzing that stops us from living.

Today, don't think. Act on your gut instincts. If you really believe that you are connected to and guided by the Light, than just let that flow right through you.

Of the angels it is written: "And their legs are a straight leg." Furthermore, it is written that people should seek to be like angels. But in trying to emulate angels, how should you understand this teaching about a "straight leg?"

Actually, the teaching refers to the fact that angels move straight ahead. An angel doesn't look right or left, either literally or figuratively. In other words, angels are unaffected by what is said or thought about them. Nothing deters an angel, and this is the level you should desire to reach in your spiritual work.

How can you reach this level? It's a matter of performing the actions you know to be the correct ones, rather than succumbing to the influence of other people. It means not saying only those things you think others want to hear. Pay attention today to how often the words that come out of your mouth hinge upon the opinion of others.

Today is the anniversary of the death of the great Kabbalist, Rav Yonatan ben Uziel (the Amouka). He is known for his power to unite soul mates.

The story goes that he was so focused on spiritual study that not only did he not marry but he couldn't even understand the importance of sharing his life with another person. Once he left this world, he realized the tremendous opportunity he passed up by not seeking out his soul mate and he vowed to help anyone who asked him to find their soul mate.

While I want to inspire you to connect to this righteous soul on the day of his passing, I also want to share with you a deeper lesson.

On a certain level, you and I make the same mistake every day of our lives. We don't recognize the tremendous Light that can be revealed in our every relation and interaction with other people. We say things like, "I can't deal with you right now, I am working on myself," or, "I am in the midst of my own craziness, let's talk another time." But this misses the point that the most important spiritual work is the work we do with others.

Today—and every day—I urge you to give a second look at all the people in your life. Appreciate the amount of Light you can reveal in a conversation with a good friend, a deep discussion with a partner, or a romantic encounter with a lover.

And remember, if we weren't meant to deal with human beings, we'd each be born on an island—all alone.

Don't put people into categories.

Three people could tell me the same thing, but I will take one more seriously than the others just because of the way they look. I catch myself doing this all the time. It's an unconscious response. Some would say it's human nature, but as a student and teacher of spirituality, I'm all about overcoming my human nature, and tapping into my higher nature.

> *"Respect everyone without focusing on, and being influenced by, their external appearance."*
> —Rav Berg

We know this isn't easy. But it's so worth it to look past the physical illusion, and respect everyone.

Today, stop putting people into boxes. Give them a chance. You never know who the Light chose to be a messenger for you. And don't forget, they are doing the same thing for you.

When a person looks for something negative, he will always find it—and then he'll pass it on. We could have 1000 happy customers, but you can bet we'll only hear about the three that were unhappy.

Why isn't it as easy to find the good? Why don't we gossip about the good things that people do or say?

Today, first focus on how hard it is to resist seeking out what is wrong with people. Then, practice spotting the good things you see. It will make your life a lot more pleasurable (and less full of headaches).

We each come to this world with a soul mission. However, most of us leave this world without ever having accomplished that mission.

We return back "upstairs" and realize we had our sights set on all the wrong things. If we are lucky, we get a chance to start over and come back again.

Why not get it right this time around? You don't want to go through the terrible twos again, do you? And puberty? I don't think so.

Why are you alive? What did your soul come here to do? These are worthy questions to ask of yourself today. Too bad we can't just Google what our life mission is. Maybe someday. But for now, the best way to find the answer is to ask the question. Ask enough times—and with intensity—and you will start seeing signs pointing you in the right direction.

One illusion in life that gets us into lots of trouble is the feeling that there isn't enough good stuff to go around.

It's like watching your favorite dessert being sliced before your eyes and everyone's reaching in for a big, thick piece, and it's still nowhere near your turn. You start thinking you're going to be left out, so you quickly come up with strategies to make sure you definitely get your share.

Most of our daily thoughts involve getting ours and keeping someone else from getting theirs.

Now imagine the relief you'd feel if the waiter walked out of the kitchen carrying two more trays of dessert, fresh out of the oven, and announced that there were several more baking. You'd realize then that there was more than enough for everybody. And you'd realize that there was no need to expend all that energy on stressing over your slice, the size of it, the quality, and the order in which you received it. You could have relaxed and just enjoyed yourself the whole time.

Keep working, moving forward, sharing, and caring about the people who cross your path. You'll get your slice in due time. The harder you work for it, the tastier it'll be.

June / July

In my brother Michael's New Moon of Capricorn Web video, he made an analogy to the ego that is especially appropriate this month. Imagine a wild man with a stick chasing you down the street and you sit down and allow him to clobber you. Our negative thoughts are that wild man and when we wallow in them, we are acting as accomplices in our own abuse.

If we only understood the profundity of this idea, we'd get up and run!

Today, do what you have to do to get out of a negative state of mind. Understand that your Opponent is your thoughts, not the people who are ticking you off.

Kabbalists say when you are experiencing anxiety, it is your potential self pushing you to your next level. It's called *Or Makif* (Surrounding Light).

Your Surrounding Light doesn't come to you to ruin your day. It comes to help you and tell you what you need to do next. But like a child who isn't heard, it has to get your attention somehow.

Today, ask your fear what it wants. Yes, you can talk to it. But the key is to be gentle, to be patient, and to not expect an answer right away.

Once you learn to talk to your anxiety, and listen to its messages, practice hearing what it wants for you. If it wants you to start dating, allow your body to experience what it would feel like to be on a really good date. If it wants you to look for a new job, experience what it would feel like to be working at your dream job. By resonating out that energy there, you will attract the right situation to match your vibrations.

One *Pesach*, I spoke about the cave. To one degree or another, we are afraid of what people will think of us and our secret thoughts, so we hide in a cave. We are so terrified that someone will find out we are not as witty or pretty as we play ourselves off to be.

Find someone today with whom to break the barrier. Choose a person you are purposely keeping distant from for fear that they will find you out. Take a step toward one person you are not close with for fear of what they will think of you.

Accept yourself. You can't embrace the Light of others if you can't embrace your own.

Cause and Effect this, Cause and Effect that—the words are constantly buzzing in our ears. But do they penetrate? Usually not. How can they if we are not built to see the effects of our actions? It's not logical to always be considering the bigger picture.

Fortunately, kabbalists are not logical.

The *Zohar* explains that the spiritual world and the physical world are always connected. We always have a foot in both worlds. Our task, illogical and impossible as it may seem, is to constantly remember we are facing the Creator every moment of our lives.

Today, rather than observing yourself, as I usually suggest, spend time watching others. Imagine what the effects of their actions and words might be. I promise you the thoughts will be scary, if not awe-inspiring. My intention is to increase your awareness of your OWN actions and words.

Remember, just observe. Don't say a word.

When your tire blows on the freeway and you forgot your wallet at the office, it's easy to think the Light abandoned you. But the Light never abandons you, even when you feel totally alone. The Light simply puts you in situations that you can learn from. In fact, when you think it's not there is when it's there the most.

Apply this lesson to your next difficult situation. Talk to the Light. Ask it what it wants you to learn.

I don't know about you, but it seems everywhere I go I hear people complaining about one thing or another.

Kabbalah explains that complaining is all about wanting to fill a desire without having to work for it. We want to say what's wrong and have the situation automatically redress itself. It's a consciousness of thinking things should come to us simply because we're dissatisfied.

But we all know there are no free lunches in life. Complaining goes against the nature of the Universe because the Universal Rule is: If we want something, we have to put effort into it. If we don't work for something, the fulfillment we get will disappear.

If we want to have something, we have to take responsibility.

Now, don't go getting complaining and constructive criticism confused. The difference between the two is the "taking responsibility" part. When we criticize constructively, we usually provide suggestions—we're in the mind-set of contributing to make it better.

What's your biggest complaint today? Find one action you can take that will lend to the improvement of the situation.

It's so easy to spot what others need to change, isn't it?

It's even easy to point it out to them.

But it's not so easy to give people the freedom they need to access the truth on their own. We think people can't see what's wrong with themselves. But, as we know, we judge ourselves more than we judge others.

If there is someone in your life who just isn't "getting it," find a way to support and validate them. And if your instincts are crying out to give them a dose of cold hard truth, make sure you ladle it out with sensitivity and heart. Without that, you will only make them feel worse. And then they won't get it at all.

Most of us favor to feel like a victim to life's injustices. Yet still, some of us choose to transform life's supreme difficulties into supreme blessings. This is the spiritual path.

The spiritual path leads you to jump outside yourself when you're obsessing. The spiritual path leads you to look around and to focus on someone else's pain. The spiritual path leads you to do something about it.

If you find your outlook overwhelmed by uncertainty, then do the following today:

SHARE – Go outside of yourself; help and think of others.

GET CLARITY – You are not your feelings. Just because you are feeling blue doesn't mean that you are blue. Feelings are fickle. Resist holding on to them too tightly.

There is a story of a righteous man who is asked to curse another man. He is told that the person in question is evil and wants to hurt everyone. The righteous man replies, "Instead of cursing him, wouldn't it be easier to bless him so that he'll be able only to see the Light? If he can only see the Light, the rest will be taken care of, won't it?"

Today, bless the people you want to curse. You can't fight darkness with darkness. You have to fight it with Light.

Kabbalists have no guilt.

Why? Because they understand that when we continually beat ourselves up for a mistake we made, we're just feeding our Opponent. In order to move on in our lives, we have to forgive ourselves.

OK, we said something stupid, we hurt someone's feelings, we disappointed a friend. What good does it do to keep reliving it? The best thing to do is to laugh about it, and think about how you can do it different next time.

By letting go of self-hate and injecting humor, our ego gets ripped to shreds and we remove the judgment from the action.

Let yourself off the hook today.

When you get closer to the Light, you are more susceptible to short-circuiting.

As you grow spiritually, you expand your Vessel and that makes you want more. It's good to want more —to want more success, to want more achievement. But when you increase your Vessel and capacity, negative things you once got away with are not acceptable to you anymore.

Think of it this way: When you're three years old, it's not a big deal to take your clothes off in the middle of a crowded room. But you can't do it when you're twenty, can you? The same goes for spirituality—there are things you once did that you just can't do anymore because they will leave you feeling empty.

What old behaviors are you dipping into, to your detriment?

Kabbalah explains you don't get a drop more of life than you can handle.

When you come to a place where you say you can't take it anymore, that's good! Don't TAKE it anymore. GIVE. Expand your way of thinking, your Vessel, your ability to have, so that you can rise to the occasion.

What occasion in your life do you want to rise to? How can you empower yourself to be all you can be?

It is written that when the Kotzker Rebbe was on his deathbed, all his students gathered around him and asked, "Master, please tell us, what was the most important thing you did in your life?" The kabbalist thought for a moment and answered, "What I am doing this very minute."

What does this teach us? Thinking about the past or worrying about the future is a waste of time. It only takes us away from the importance of the moment we're in.

Today, be present in whatever it is you are doing. It is the most important thing you have ever done. Today, when you are obsessing about what you'll do the next hour for lunch, for dinner, for life, set your obsessions aside and just enjoy the moment. Put all your thoughts into right now. Right now is bliss. Right now.

"*There is anger, and there is anger.*"
— The *Zohar*

The *Zohar* says there are two sides to anger, "one blessed and the other cursed."

At times, we must exercise judgment or anger that is rooted in love and sharing. We call this positive anger; it is a form of love, as when a parent disciplines a child out of concern for the child's safety.

Ego-based anger, however, creates negative energy. If a parent punishes a child as an expression of inner frustration, this anger is cursed. One version of anger generates love; the other creates darkness. Today, dole out anger rooted in love. Bless it with the Light of the Creator.

I hope I'm not the only one doing some writing. Journaling our thoughts, fears, desires, schemes, regrets, and fantasies is a powerful spiritual guide.

Are you up for a quick writing exercise today?

Make a list of your desires. Put down everything that comes to mind no matter how small or how foolish it may seem: Going skiing with your best friend this weekend, that your sister stops doing drugs, that your children stop fighting, to be a famous singer, to end world hunger, to save people's lives, to make so much money your parents never have to work again…

Just put that desire down on paper. When you've done that, write next to each desire how you think you might feel if you attained it. How might your life change?

Without knowing your true desires, you don't stand much of a chance at attaining them. So be honest!

There is a spiritual law that dictates that whoever cares about others is cared about by the Creator. And if we know that we are nothing without the care of the Light, then it is impossible not to care about others.

If we spend our entire lives dealing with ourselves alone, then we won't have even the slightest chance of making it, not unlike a snowflake in Hell.

Today, assess how much time you spend helping yourself, versus time you spend genuinely reaching out and helping others.

Today starts off the twenty-one most challenging days of the year. These three weeks are known by kabbalists as *yamim ben hametzarim*, roughly translated as "days of narrowness."

How appropriate, then, that the lyrics of a Citizen Cope song continually pop up on my iTunes shuffe:

> "... *but what you've done here is put yourself between a bullet and a target.*"

Basically, these are the days of being between a bullet and a target. This narrowness translates into difficult people, drawn-out processes, and drama. Did I mention *drama*? And to top it all off, during the next 10 days, Mercury is in retrograde, which means communication is jumbled and misread. This begs the question, "What kind of all-loving God would intentionally arrange the universe this way?"

The kind that wants us to earn our fulfillment. The next time you find yourself running away from a difficult person or situation, know that you're actually running away from your own fulfillment.

I was reading something my brother, Michael, had written a long time ago. It's such an important lesson to keep fixed in our minds that I'd like to share it with you now:

> Our spiritual work is not to draw the Light of the Creator to us—His Light always flows to us—but rather, to remove the barriers that we have erected between the Creator's Light and ourselves.
>
> The best way to make ourselves capable of receiving the Creator's Light is through acts of sharing. There is a spiritual law that as we act, so does the Creator act toward us. When we act with mercy and give to others, we awaken mercy and giving from above.

I could send you daily tune-ups from here to eternity, but this is really all you need to know. It's the essence of life and Kabbalah. As we act, so does the Creator act toward us.

End of the month. Money is tight. Charges on the credit card are increasing. Rent is due. Tuition for schools is due, too. The news gets funkier every day. The month of Cancer can be a downer. On and on and on...

What do we do?

Pray! Pray for the ability to acknowledge that God is in everything.

We all have blessings in our lives, even if we're having trouble finding a husband or making money or getting our lives on track or battling illness. Even when life seems at its darkest, there's always a pilot Light burning.

Today, look for that Light. Count your blessings, as they say. What are you thankful for, right now, right this second?

I have a message that my father and teacher, the Rav, wishes to share with the world:

> *"If we are not able to live peacefully with each other, why should we think that it is possible to make peace between the Arabs and the Israelis?"*

I think the challenge my father is presenting to us is clear. We need to step up our efforts at treating people with human dignity if this situation in the Middle East is ever going to change. It means you need to find a way to love that guy, whom you hate, sitting next to you. It means smiling at the lady who cuts you off on the highway instead of giving her the finger. It means if we have nothing nice to say, say nothing at all.

I know this seems like a bit of a strong message, but we must all remember that we are in the three most negative weeks of the year and the time for nice words and "inspirational" messages is over. It's do-or-die time.

Lately, I have been talking about the importance of getting along with one another. I think it is a point worth repeating at this time. Conflict and war among nations begins with friction between individual people. A nation at war is simply the effect of spiritual darkness born of animosity and intolerance among individuals who comprise the nation. As long as brothers or friends can find reason to clash with one another, nations will devise reasons for bloody battle.

Choose one person you are holding a grudge against and forgive them. "But you don't know what he did to me…" Forgive him, anyway. You're only hurting yourself—and the world—by holding on to the hate.

There is actually tremendous Light available in these three difficult weeks, but the problem is there is no filter to protect us from it. It's like having no ozone layer to shield us from the sun. Usually, we have screens that determine how much Light we can receive, but now we're getting it in overabundance.

How can we keep from short-circuiting? To tap into the energy in a balanced way, we basically have to remain low-key, stay involved in spirituality, and do small acts of sharing. Be less self-involved and more involved with others.

As tough as the three negative weeks can be, during this time there are amazing opportunities for gaining clarity.

The *Zohar* says that you can get insights into where your life needs to go. Maybe it's time to rethink your career, or become more spiritual, or get out of a bad relationship. The Light is showing you new things and awakening you to those closed-off parts of yourself.

These kernels of truth will come from unexpected places. Be open. Don't hold on so tightly to your notions of what should be. Remember, it's not about you; it's about the Light. Ask the Light to show you what you can't see.

It's a funny thing, this time of year. On one hand, the kabbalists advise against planting any new seeds, starting new business ventures, signing contracts, and so on.

At the same time, the mental chatter is incessant, regarding what to do and what to change about our lives—break up, get married, buy, sell, quit, fire, hire.

The trick is to know that it is our Opponent who is urging us to plant these seeds, and if we do so we're sabotaging ourselves. We must realize that if we do what that voice is telling us, our Opponent won't need to work for the rest of the year. By planting his seeds now, we're paving the way for a challenge-laden future.

So for the next week, until next Tuesday night, resist the thoughts that urge you to action. Hold on to all of your bright ideas and let them percolate. Resisting the impulse to act will result in much more positive outcomes in the near future.

You know, I think these three negative weeks get a bad rap. Personally, this is a productive time of year for me as there is so much truth revealed. All the cobwebs of self-delusion are cleared and I can see where my ego is hiding.

Another great thing about this time is I learn who my real friends are. When things get a bit heavy, I notice that some friends run to me and others run away. That's the real test of friendship.

Of course, the flip side is we have to be willing to take responsibility for our share. We want others to feel our pain, but are we there when it's tough for them? How many of us drop friends because "they're too negative?" Who among us is willing to go into the depths of hell to pull a friend out of addiction, or depression, or co-dependency? It takes strength to go to someone else's black hole.

That is the strength we must gather today, to pick someone up when they are falling. Choose one close friend who is craving love and channel it to them. Give your agenda a time-out. Just focus on what your friend needs, and on what pain is driving them to self-destructive actions.

New York's Grand Central Terminal experienced an explosion in July of 2007. Fortunately, it was only a transformer that malfunctioned and no one was hurt. But for a moment many thought it was a terrorist attack and my inbox was flooded with requests for prayers.

This got me thinking about something my mother and teacher, Karen Berg, said recently:

> *"The greatest plague that exists in this world is apathy. Somebody else is sick, somebody else is in need, somebody else is dying. 'So what? I have my comfort' We only care when it hits us."*

We are all guilty of this. But if we want to prevent future attacks or any type of chaos from touching us, then we must start to look up and see the pain and deprivation and lack that exists. And we must do something about it.

How can you get involved today? How can your conscious thought, your energy, your love, and your compassion stem the flow of pain that is currently washing over the world?

Science and Kabbalah agree: The greater the resistance, the greater the Light that is revealed. And whether you're talking about the light in a light bulb or the Lightforce of the Creator, that universal truth is the same.

Especially in these three weeks, resistance needs to be the first—if not the only—thing on our minds.

Translation: Those problems you're running away from—you're running in the wrong direction. Go towards them. Embrace them. That's where your fulfillment is hiding.

Today, pick one thing you've been avoiding and face it. Have the strength to hear what's painful, to do what's uncomfortable, and to feel what's unpleasant.

You'll be surprised by the results.

Have you ever seen those warnings, "Identity Theft—Don't Be a Victim?" They're actually quite kabbalistic.

We think we are who we are. Meaning, we think we are these notions we have of ourselves—black, white, man, woman, secure, insecure, lawyer, actor, son, brother, ADD, OCD, happy-go-lucky, whatever. But most of the time, we are totally clueless about our real identity.

On a soul level, we transcend categories and mental constructs. We are souls, pure sparks of the Creator. In everyday language: We are love. We are compassion. We are giving. We are groundless. We are limitless. And, of course, we are one. You, me, and everyone reading this, everyone walking around in your office, or on the street, or wherever you are reading this, we're all connected.

Today, know that whoever you think you are, you are not. Ask for guidance to be shown the real you. Reclaim your identity.

I've got an unusual request today. Do something that's just for you. Enjoy yourself.

We are going through a tough time (the Three Negative Weeks). There's a lot of judgment flying around in our heads. And it's OK to find little pleasures that make us happy. Sometimes, indulging in a favorite snack, or taking an extra ten minutes on our lunch hour, or going to the beach instead of the gym, is just what we need to put a smile back on our faces.

Do something for yourself today, guilt-free. If you're not happy, then none of us is happy.

July / August

Would you rather be happy or right today? Life is not about who's right and who's wrong. Life is only about becoming the creator of your own fulfillment by finding the hidden Light. You do that each time you share with someone. That's the rule of the game.

If someone wrongs you and you react, you aren't sharing. You might be right, but you also just hung up a curtain in the process. That's what nobody in this world seems to understand. They haven't figured that one out yet. And that's why the world is awash in sorrow and pain.

Today, ask yourself this: Would you rather be right—and miserable? Or would you rather be wrong—and happy?

If you've been reading communications from The Kabbalah Centre, you're accustomed to our signature phrase, "The Best Kept Secret: Wisdom to tranform your life!"

Well, I've got another one: Patience. This is a big secret. HUGE.

It goes like this: Some kind of crisis leads us to walk down the spiritual path. At first, because we are so low and humble, we are grateful for any love that comes our way. As we start walking faster, with more confidence in our stride, we become familiar with the landscape of miracles, and we know there are goodies coming our way so long as we keep walking.

After a while, we get impatient for the goodies, as if we are owed something in a timelier manner. We study the *Zohar* and then we look up, expecting our soul mate to jump on the bus. We donate money and we expect a raise in our next paycheck. We become impatient with God.

Patience is giving God room to do God's work. It's knowing that we'll get what we deserve when the time is right. That time could be any time at all.

Today, forget about the result. Just put in the work, send your wishes and prayers into the Universe. And don't worry, God is listening. The things you are looking for will all be found in due time.

Judging from e-mails I've been getting from students, there are some of us who feel like we have never experienced "the Light."

Let me tell you that you have. We all have, even though it may be fleeting.

Think of the moment you put the final touches on a project that you fiercely believed in—one that took lots of time and effort to complete. That rush from a job well done is the Light.

Or how about that time you thought of someone and they called just at that moment? That, too, is the Light. Or when you get a great idea, or answer. That, too, is the Light.

So you have tou   Light. And the more you are aware of it   will.

Today, find   ou do. It's there. Allow yo

Have

Tune-Ups

Red String. If there's one thing everyone knows about The Kabbalah Centre, it's that we teach the importance of wearing it in order to protect ourselves from the evil eye. I'm certainly not going to be able to explain this seemingly archaic concept in a few paragraphs. But for those of you who have been studying and wearing it, you know its powers.

I was reading this week in one of the ancient texts that "fish do not have evil eye because they are completely surrounded by water."

OK, that's a little weird. Who ever thinks of fish getting or giving the evil eye? But the kabbalistic meaning of this concept is that water is *Chesed* (mercy). What I want to share with you about this is that when we immerse ourselves in the waters of a sharing consciousness by caring about others, the jealousy of other people has no effect on us.

Be merciful today. Cut people some slack. Smile at people like you're smiling at chubby little babies.

If the vise in your head has been a little too tight these last three weeks, I've got good news.

Today is the anniversary of Rav Isaac Luria (the Ari), the 16th century Kabbalist who codified the immense secrets of life into what is now referred to as Lurianic Kabbalah (the system we teach and practice here at The Kabbalah Centre).

The Ari's wisdom, and Kabbalah itself, are based upon the following concept: The only way to achieve true joy and fulfillment is to become a being of sharing.

We know that studying the wisdom of Kabbalah means using it, and using it means sharing. Now we have the extraordinary opportunity to store up those reserves that fortify our sharing capabilities throughout the year.

Today, our modus operandi is: Share, share, share, share, and share!

Today, I want you to let go, but we say the phrase "let go" so often that it has lost its meaning to many. Allow me to clarify what this means: To let go is to fear less and to love more. It's as simple and as difficult as that.

A husband goes to the doctor and says, "I have a big problem with my wife. She doesn't want to admit she is deaf." The doctor tells him, "There is a simple test. When you get to the doorstep, scream, 'Honey, what's for dinner?' If there is no answer, move closer a few steps and ask again. Move another step closer, and then another, until she answers."

The husband comes home, stops at the door, and yells out, "Honey, what's for dinner?" Silence. He takes another step and asks again; still no answer. He is within a few inches when he screams, "Honey, what's for dinner?!" She turns to him and says, "I answered you four times. We are having soup!"

The faults we see in others are quite often things we can't bear to see in ourselves. Think about this today. Look at the annoying behaviors of others and ask yourself, "Is that what I'm like?"

Time is money.

Imagine a genie that pops out of your computer screen every day and grants you a million dollars. The only condition is, you've got to spend it by the time your head hits the pillow that night. This is how the Creator doles out life to us. Every hour is a chance to learn something new, every minute a rung to climb, every second a fleeting moment to tackle your soul's correction (*tikkun*).

Spend your time wisely today. Offer valid until.... Who knows when?

Today, let us all reflect on the essence of why we are alive:

"We have come here for only one reason: To see how we are going to deal with our fellow man. It's not about how righteous we will be—throw that out. It is about where our consciousness lies with our fellow man. This is the most critical task of humanity."
—Rav Berg

Bottom line: If people were perfect, they'd be easy to love. But they're not. And that's the whole point.

Today—and every day—no matter how justified you are in judging or striking back, I beg of you to heed the spiritual battle cry of my father and teacher, Rav Berg.

The future of humanity depends on it.

We all have a tendency to write people off when they bother us. Not just any people. The ones closest to us. Sons not talking to mothers, brothers estranged from sisters, best friends at war. If only we realized that our negative actions don't define who we are, then we'd have more tolerance for each other.

We are all works in progress, and along with all the wonderful things we do comes the junk. But the sign of a real relationship is if we give even when we're not getting.

Today, focus on one close relationship that puts your love to the test and extend generosity to that person—without looking for something in return.

I always recommend walking away from heated situations. Not long ago, I received some feedback from readers saying, "OK, I walked away but I am still furious. Why does restricting my reactive behavior feel like I am repressing my emotions?"

It feels like that because you haven't finished restricting. True restriction requires two steps: First, stopping the knee-jerk reaction and then, transforming your judgment into mercy. Managing the first step is difficult, so it is good if you have gotten that far. I wish I could tell you otherwise, but the next step requires just as much effort.

If you want to stop hugging your chaos, as my father and teacher, the Rav, says, you've got to be willing to let go of being right. This means feeling the other person's pain instead of calculating how wrong they are. Ask yourself what pain—in this lifetime or beyond—is causing them to act this way. The kabbalists say that just by asking yourself, "What's going on with him?" you generate energy that will help the other person!

Ultimately, we want to change so that we can be closer to the Light, closer to our fulfillment. That kind of change requires yearning for a big desire. Yes, kabbalists speak of desiring desire. The greater the yearning, the more Light we receive.

In your quiet time today, ask the Light to give you the desire to have desire. This is something to think deeply about.

A child learns to walk by falling down and standing up again. Measured against a lifetime of walking, this period of continual stumbling is relatively short.

Similarly, the hardships and afflictions in our lives are relatively short. They are sent to help us learn to walk in the ways of the Light. When we understand our afflictions in this way, we realize that their duration is brief compared to a lifetime of spiritual fulfillment.

On the other hand, when life appears strangely calm and placid, the Light may be delaying judgments against us for self-centered behavior. We should be wary of our connection to the Light during these moments and begin to reflect on our lives with humility and a sincere desire to change.

What are two of the greatest obstacles to love?

Impatience and intolerance.

Instead of feverishly attempting to impose our opinions on our wives, boyfriends, partners, and friends, it is better to join hands with people who think
differently from us, and together bring blessing and benefit to all humanity.

Today, let the words of Rav Berg guide you: "Removing fragmentation from human experience requires abolishing hatred toward all those whose opinions are different from our own."

Tonight begins the holiday of *Tu B'Av*, known as the kabbalistic Valentine's Day. It is the one day of the year when the forces of the universe are specifically tuned into the soul mate frequency. This is why our sages stated there is no happier day in the year.

It doesn't necessarily mean you are going to meet "the one" today (though it has happened). What it does mean is your existing relationships can grow stronger, provided that you create an opening for this day's energy to enter. That opening is the opening of your heart. Unconditional love.

Unconditional love is not as lofty as it sounds. It's quite practical and down-to-earth, actually. It means loving instead of judging, loving without an agenda, loving when you don't feel like loving.

Practice unconditional loving today. When you feel yourself getting annoyed or angry with someone, switch it up and decide to emanate love. Let it flow out and it will eventually find its way back in.

Staying with yesterday's theme of soul mates, I've got a question for you: How do we know if we are with our soul mate?

The great 16th century Kabbalist, Rav Isaac Lurai (the Ari), wrote that you can know for sure if the other person comes to you from a faraway country. "A faraway country" is code for overcoming a great space that separates people. And that space is the *Desire to Receive for the Self Alone* (ego).

A real soul mate relationship is one in which two people give to each other completely. Their interest is not in receiving anything for themselves.

Now you see why the Ari said a faraway country. Changing our nature from taker to giver is as difficult as crossing the Great Plains, or the Atlantic, or the Sahara, or whatever geographical reference speaks to you.

Today, realize that all the relationships in your life have the potential to be soul mate-worthy. The more you focus on the other person, on what they might need in any given moment, the closer you will come to revealing the deeper, most beautiful aspects of your bond.

We have to stop thinking backwards. We have to realize that many of us think we care about someone because we love them. In reality, true, unconditional love works entirely the opposite way: We must care for the person in order to love them.

Most of us operate with the agenda that "I will love you so you will care about me." We're not looking for any sort of giving or stretching on our part. Rather, it's all about how we can get attention, get love, get our needs met. When love is entirely conditional, it will be subject to the conditions of life. Whereas when you care for someone, truly care for their well-being first, you'll start to love them regardless of what happens.

Kabbalah teaches we have two images: Who we are, and who we can be. Who we can be is where we want to be. It's our potential. It's where our mind goes when we're asked, "If you could be anything, what would it be?"

Where does your mind go when you read that question? Can you allow yourself to imagine a perfect you?

Today, envision the evolved you. The more you do it, the faster you will evolve.

I know a lot of single people who are avoiding relationships because of bad past experiences. As painful as love-gone-sour can be, it's important to remember a fundamental kabbalistic teaching: The universe is a mirror reflecting back to you everything you put into it.

If you want to use a painful experience, such as a breakup, to help you grow, you must see the event as it truly is—a lesson, not a punishment. When you learn the lesson, you are relieved of the suffering, and Light and joy come into your life.

Whether or not you are currently with someone, choose one relationship that ended in flames and ask yourself what invaluable life lesson you learned as a result.

Do you see the truth in people?

The secret is not to see yourself within others, but rather to see others within yourself. When you treat people as if they were part of your own flesh and blood, you are better able to identify with them, to know their truth, and to offer them compassion.

Imagine everyone you meet today is YOU. Put yourself in your own shoes.

> *"When you believe it, then you will see it."*
> —Rav Berg

Yesterday, we looked at past relationships. Today, let us look at current ones. If you are struggling in any relationship—with a lover, friend, parent, or child—you ought to know that you are being offered a great chance for happiness. If you approach your difficulties from the perspective of a victim, then you will experience no growth. But if you look inside, and are honest with yourself, you will realize that your relationship is merely reflecting a part of yourself which you don't like. By working on yourself and transforming that flawed, negative aspect of your character—which is what drew the situation to you in the first place— you remove the need to experience the situation in the future.

Think about one person in your life with whom you're disgusted. What aspect of yourself are you seeing in them?

We've talked about past and present relationships. Let's be proactive and discuss the future. The type of people you'll draw into your life down the road depends on your energy today. Remember the law of affinity: Like attracts like. If you're a grouch, you'll attract grouches. If you're critical, you'll attract critics. You see where I am going with this.

Be the kind of person you want to be with. This applies to current relationships, as well. If you don't like the people in your life, you are the one who has to change, not them.

Today I want you to focus on one person in your life whose behavior is getting under your skin. Identify the behavior. Now look at yourself—how are you behaving in a similar fashion?

In the teachings of the great Kabbalist, Rav Ashlag, founder of The Kabbalah Centre, he made it clear that the *Desire to Receive for the Self Alone* is the source of all our troubles. Rav Ashlag said:

> *"I speak for so long about the Desire to Receive being a klipah (external shell that steals our Light), and they don't believe me, since if they would have believed me, they certainly would have cast away this Desire to Receive."*

The main spiritual labor, in the eyes of Rav Ashlag, was changing the nature ingrained in us, turning it around and using it to benefit someone else. About this Rav Ashlag would say: *"The measured amount of labor input by a person must be given in one charge, with the greatest energy."* Rav Ashlag often used a parable to explain this principle: If a person wants to break down a piece of board from a table with his fist, he must strike it and apply the fullest weight of the force in one charge, because if he would draw out this energetic force into a slower pace over a longer time, little by little, his striking hits would never break it.

There are many meanings to be found within these words, but for me, the most important message is: Act now. Today, I challenge you to apply your "fullest weight" to every action you take, no matter how seemingly insignificant.

Think about the number of different people there are in the world—billions of them. Imagine the creativity it took to make each and every person different. Even identical twins are not exactly alike. We all look different because we all bring a different energy to the world, and we're all needed. We all express another piece of the bigger puzzle.

The only way to appreciate our power is by putting our maximum effort into everything we do. That's the only way to know how special we are.

Today, think of one area where you are not living up to your fullest potential. Is there something you can do to change that?

Anxiety is internal. It feels real, but it's not.

Many of us are our own worst enemy because of our unkind belief systems about who we think we are —and are not. We don't accept ourselves, both the Light and the dark. Somehow, we should be better, should be more like someone else, should be further ahead.

To quote *The Deer Hunter,* "*This is this, this ain't something else, THIS IS THIS!*"

You have a deep, spiritual soul that has the capacity for unconditional love. The first and most important love is self-love; everything flows downstream from there.

Today, give yourself the gift of unconditional love.

A man visits the hardware store, looking for a certain-sized nail. He is told they are in aisle three, third floor, in the back. He goes there, but can't find the nails. He runs back to the clerk, "Excuse me, I didn't find it there." "Oh, you mean those nails: Aisle seven, in the basement." The man goes; still no nails. He returns again to the clerk, "Do you even sell these nails?"

The clerk says, "Oh, those nails. They are right here."

"Why did you make me run up and down the entire store?!"

"They are the most popular item in the store. If they were easy to get, we would run out of stock. We have to make sure the customer really wants them."

This is the game the Light plays with us.

Today, ask yourself, "Do I really want to elevate? Do I really want my life to be different? How much work am I willing to put in so that my life will be chaos-free?"

Mercy and judgment.

Which word resonates more? Perhaps you need to get better acquainted with the other. Kabbalah teaches that in our waking lives we operate out of these two basic modes. Some of us are too merciful with people (read: Doormats); others of us are too judgmental with people (read: Steamrollers).

If you find yourself getting taken advantage of time and again, then be tougher with people. Set boundaries. Stand up for yourself. Be courageous. If you find yourself giving people the business most of the day, then chill out a little. You don't need to police people. See past people's faults, into their pain. Have compassion. And throw some your own way because chances are you are judging simply because the reflection in the mirror is too ugly to bear.

Nothing is 100 percent black or white, right or wrong, good or bad.

When you look at reality and say, "I am right," you should know that there is always someone who will come along and say you are wrong. The problem with argument is not who is right or who is wrong—it is that you think that you are right and someone else is wrong!

Be open to another point of view today, even when you are sure you are 100 percent right.

What does "sending energy" mean?

It means when there is someone in your life to whom you are particularly sensitive, you spend extra time quietly visualizing an encounter with this person in a tolerant, proactive, compassionate way.

Try this. Literally picture this person in your mind. See the words coming out of your mouth. Imagine their facial reactions.

If life is a movie, then this is writing your script for the next encounter.

Here's a look on the brighter side: Kabbalah teaches us that life provides countless opportunities, much like a multiplex cinema. And you're the star on every screen. What's more, each theater shows a different quality film. In Theater One, you're living your ideal movie, where blessings and joy abound. In Theater Twelve (actually, the number of potential movies is infinite), your life is, for lack of a better term, a horror flick.

While the Lightforce of the Creator is always the producer, you are always the director. You make the choices that determine how the plot twists and turns. You're also the casting director, choosing who is playing each part.

I share this with you so that from now on, you take every decision in your life as one that can rewrite the script of your movie. This doesn't mean that every decision must be a drama. But whether you're choosing between right or left, chocolate or vanilla, Los Angeles or New York, know that you, and only you, get to decide what happens in the next scene.

August / September

Welcome to the new month of Virgo. The most amazing thing about this time of year is we get to see all of our garbage. Everything that's wrong with us starts shooting to the surface, and the more we want to see it, the more it will appear.

Why is this good? On *Rosh Hashanah*, we can hit the refresh button on our lives only if we clean the corrupted files already stored there.

But enough of the metaphors. The bottom line is this: Where did you go wrong last year, and how can you fix it now?

You can start by thinking of one person you hurt this year. Picture the pain they went through and feel it as if it were your own.

Yesterday, I wrote about cleansing yourself in preparation for the New Year (*Rosh Hashanah*). I must warn you that your internal Opponent will make you feel that whatever is wrong with you isn't so bad. It will trick you into thinking the problems you are experiencing are better than what would happen if you changed. It will do everything in its power to stop you from seeing your flaws.

Today, ask a trusted friend, "What's the one thing I need to change this year?" When the anger or fear or doubt comes up, remember what I said. It's your Opponent talking. See beyond it and imagine what life would be like if you did make that change.

Today, you'll have to work for the wisdom. You'll understand why tomorrow. Pick someone close to you—friend, lover, child—and write a list of everything that bugs you about that person.

Just take a few seconds and jot it down on a scrap of paper or on your computer. Keep it to yourself and tomorrow I'll have you do something with it.

Did you do yesterday's exercise? To recap, I asked you to think of someone close to you—friend, lover, child—and write a list of everything that bugs you about them.

Today, I would like you to think about which of these aspects you have within you. For sure they're there, even if the other person has it 200 times worse. You wouldn't be able to see it if you didn't. If you spot it, you got it.

Be open to changing in yourself what you'd like to see changed in others.

Spiritual growth involves not only accepting our garbage but our gifts as well.

The minute we start to see a little bad, we think it's all bad. That's the Opponent's handiwork. It tells us, "Ah, you're a compulsive giver, so it's better if you didn't give at all. Then you'd really be working on yourself." The only thing that line of thinking accomplishes is keeping you from your job—from revealing Light.

The energy of Virgo is here to pilot us back towards our God-given gifts, to push us to really believe in them.

What's your gift? Are you a good listener? A great motivator? A hard worker? Focus on one and allow it to come out today. Put the doubts on the shelf and trust yourself. Let the world see who you really are.

This month, it is easy to see what is wrong in others. This can be a blessing or a curse. On one hand, we can help people see the error of their ways and improve their lives. On the other hand, we can easily burn them out with our words.

Pay attention to the criticism that comes out of your mouth today.

It's very easy to tell the other person what you really think of them, but it's hard—almost impossible—to take back what was said. Don't be impulsive. Reason carefully, and well. Speaking before you think can lead to many troubles. On the other hand, thinking before you speak can bring miracles and wonders.

D o you ever get overwhelmed when you think about how much you have to change?

It's for this very reason that the kabbalists say:

> *"It is better for a person to change something small and be consistent about it than to take on something more difficult for a shorter time with the intention of completing the task later."*

Many times we commit to doing something even though it's clear to us that we won't be able to complete it. All we accomplish is creating one more reason to beat ourselves up, and we score one more point for the Opponent.

The trick is to learn to commit to what we can finish and to be persistent about it. Today, focus on one small thing about yourself that you know you can change, and stick with it until you do.

You're driving to work, late for a meeting. The car in front of you is putt-putting at a turtle's pace because the driver just got a flat. Naturally, you are frustrated. But do you curse the guy for making you late, or do you try to understand why he's making you late?

In the same way, don't be angry with people who don't have the capacity to change, or share with you, or love you. It's their limitation. If they could meet your needs, they would. But right now, they can't.

Today, focus on one difficult person in your life. Understand the pain that is driving their behavior. Find a way to share with them. It could be something as simple as sending them a nice thought.

One day earlier this week, my friend was driving me home. We were waiting to make a turn onto a side street when the driver behind us got impatient and cut us off. Before he sped off, he looked right at us and started screaming, "What's wrong with you?!" This guy was furious.

I'll be honest, I just came from a difficult meeting and I wasn't feeling so hot myself. This man's anger definitely rubbed me the wrong way. But at the same time, I knew I had a choice. Let his anger roil my insides, or let it roll off my back. I think you know what I chose.

If I wasn't learning spirituality and the importance of consciousness, I could easily have absorbed his anger and passed it on to my wife and kids when I got home. The lesson for me was that the domino effect is endless. You never know whose day you are going to ruin by taking out your frustration on someone else.

Today, when you find yourself getting lit up like a switchboard, think about your choice. You can either catch the garbage being hurled at you and throw it at someone else, or you can kick it to the curb, where it belongs.

The famous line, "Love your neighbor as yourself," implies that you love yourself, right? But how many of us can say we have a genuine appreciation for who we are and what we have accomplished?

Today, keep a running list of how amazing you are and all the positive things you do. Give the self-doubt a rest for a change. Love yourself. Trust yourself. Be good to yourself. If you don't, no one else will.

And don't write it on the back of a napkin. Keep this list in a place where you can refer to it when you feel like the universe is throwing darts at you.

Here's a little story for you. Once upon a time, there was a man who treated his wife poorly. Everyone in his town knew about it, but they couldn't figure out how to help. One day, they decided to approach the town's spiritual teacher and ask him to intervene.

Later that week at a public lecture, the teacher gave a stern talk on the importance of relationships and treating one's spouse with human dignity. He went on for quite some time, really driving the point home, certain that the man knew this message was for him. After the lecture, the man came up to the teacher and said, "I hope the man you were speaking to got the message."

That man is you. That man is me.

The Creator is constantly sending us messages. They could be passed on by the stranger next to us on the subway, or the little kid standing next to us on line, or any one of the countless people crossing our paths daily. We can learn something from everyone, if we just decide to be open.

Today, listen for messages hidden in seemingly mundane exchanges.

The *Zohar* has a perfect explanation for the purpose of pain.

Just as sunlight requires physical matter to reveal its radiance, spiritual Light requires a Vessel in order to express itself. Though many people think spirituality means renouncing material existence, Kabbalah takes a very different view. Rather than meditating on a mountaintop above the fray of daily existence, we are meant to embrace the chaos of life, using it as an opportunity—as a Vessel—to reveal Light.

Those momentary flash points of character transformation ignite spiritual Light.

Today, continue to look at what pains you. Resist your urge to run away from it. Feel it. Own it. Ask it what it wants you to learn.

We've all got layers upon layers of "issues." Addiction, lack of trust, rage, unruly fears. But these layers are merely effects of an emptiness felt deep inside. Our job is to locate this core of darkness, especially in the days leading up to the New Year.

We are so involved in the material world that our emptiness feels like it needs a physical fix. We feel alone, so we seek out company. We need attention, so we hurt others. We get angry, so we lash out.

But why do we need attention? Is it because we feel worthless?

Why are we alone? Is it because we don't trust anyone?

Why are we angry? Is it because we're afraid of getting hurt?

It's up to each one of us to drill down into the black hole we need filled up this year. Spend some time today thinking about this. And know that however big the pain, there is an equal amount of joy and liberation waiting for you just behind it.

In ancient times, there existed something known as the Holy Temple. It was a sanctified place used as a portal between the physical and spiritual worlds. Within the Temple was an area only the very highest priest could enter, and only once a year. It was known as the Holy of Holies.

It's the same with us. We have parts of us that everyone sees, parts that only a few see, and one place where maybe once a year we let one person see. Maybe.

The Holy of Holies within us is where our greatest Light is revealed, but it is usually guarded by our greatest pain. That is why it is rarely visited.

In the remaining time before *Rosh Hashanah*, if we really want to take our life to the next level in the New Year, we must go to that place within where we are too afraid to go.

Think about this today. What deep pain are you avoiding feeling?

I recently heard a definition of obsession that resonated with me: Obsession is trying to make what's wrong right.

I think we've all been in friendships and romances where we've shut out that intuitive voice whispering to us, "Get out.... This is not a healthy relationship for you."

Do you hear any whispers today?

Connecting with true fulfillment requires becoming aware that everything begins with consciousness. When you move your hand, it's because you had a thought, a desire, and an intention to do so. Once you become aware of this, you'll realize that by changing your consciousness, you really can change your life, and ultimately the world.

Suppose you had the power, right now, to change anything in your life in any way you wanted. What changes would you make?

Just as hatred for no reason is the singular cause of spiritual darkness in the world, unconditional love has the power to remove even the most severe judgments decreed against humanity.

A love for others, particularly our enemies, sweetens and removes looming judgments.

One of the first principles for a spiritual human being is that the very thing we need to change most about ourselves is the one thing we never see in ourselves. If someone approaches us and says we should change x, y, and z, we won't see it and we'll find a reason to justify our actions.

That's fine the first time, but if we keep hearing the same message, well…

The drama of human existence is more than a one-act play. It's a production that encompasses many lifetimes, where profits and losses accrue according to our actions.

Therefore, forgiving those who have inflicted harm upon us really has nothing to do with the other person. Kabbalistically, the people who hurt us in life are only messengers. Everything that befalls us is a result of our prior deeds. The consequences of our actions eventually return through the activities of others, in order to help us achieve spiritual growth and correction.

The strength to display compassion and forgiveness, even when we feel it is not deserved, is stimulated by today's energy.

From a kabbalistic point of view, you can never know how the Light feels if you don't know forgiveness.

These are the three F's that come with forgiveness:

- Fearlessness: Through forgiveness, a lot of fears will vanish. The most judgmental person is the one with the most fears.

- Faithfulness: If you don't forgive, you won't trust.

- Forgetting: The advice to "forgive but not forget" is all wrong. Remembering means holding on to a grudge, which blocks the Light. How do you know that you really forgave? You forgot.

Perhaps you've had or read about a near-death experience. As commonly described, your entire life flashes before your eyes and along with it, all the opportunities you missed. The relationships you stayed in out of fear of breaking up, the times you didn't share because it was more than you wanted to give, the moments you held your tongue so you wouldn't look bad—it all comes back.

Today, I challenge you to pick one opportunity that lies before you but which you are too scared, lazy, doubtful, or uptight to go after. Write it down on a piece of paper. That's all you need to do—for now.

Yesterday, I asked you to pick one opportunity that you are not seizing. The idea is that the Light is now pushing you to get a glimpse of your potential so that come *Rosh Hashanah*, you can manifest it.

Often, we don't go for what we want because it seems impossible. When you don't have a college degree and your glimpse of greatness is of you in scrubs doing brain surgery, well, it's just not practical. There's not enough time or money. Right?

I ask you to consider two things. First, perceived lack of time and money are the major reasons we don't live our dreams. Successful people often say overcoming this false perception is the key to success. It's all about how badly we want it.

Second, the kabbalists explain that if we are going to walk five miles, we need to start with one step. We're never going to leap right to our destination (not yet, at least). But if we keep putting one foot in front of the other, we'll get there before we know it.

Today, I ask you to continue focusing on that opportunity you chose to go for. Be specific. See yourself doing it. And if the image of the life you are meant to live is blurry, now is the perfect time to sharpen your focus.

"*One must be 'as a donkey to his burden.'*"
—Rav Brandwein

What Rav Brandwein means here is a donkey works and its owner profits. He is teaching us that we must not look for rewards when we perform acts of sharing and charity. We must release the need to receive.

Today, be anonymous. Do good deeds as if no one is watching or tallying. The paradox here is only when we genuinely let go, do we get all we need. And more.

And more.

And more!

Kabbalah teaches that the pain we draw into our lives is the pain we need to help us grow.

Today, I ask you to recall a moment when someone really hurt you. I'm talking about a time in your life you wouldn't revisit if I paid you a million dollars. Remember exactly how you felt when the person hurt you.

Dig deep and ask yourself why that person appeared in your movie in the first place. Why did you cast them in that role? There is now an opening in the universe for you to really get to the bottom of things and to shed light on a truly painful part of your life.

Don't give up the ship.

I can't tell you how many successful people told me their breakthroughs came the moment after they decided not to quit, forget it, change jobs, or break up.

The problem is, we give in to pain. We can't endure it, so we submit to the feelings of worthlessness, doubt, hopelessness, and on and on and on.

Today, I ask you to have patience—with yourself. Find a way to soothe yourself, to talk kindly to yourself.

Flip it. Flip it. Flip it.

You might find that you are now seeing aspects of yourself that you don't like. That's good. No, that's great! The whole idea is the Universe wants you to find yourself a new mental CD for the New Year. You are being shown where your flaws are so you know what you need to convert in order to create that new CD.

Be open today. Be willing to see and be told about your flaws. Be certain that recognizing the problem is the secret of the solution.

What goal—physical or spiritual—are you working toward?

Do you see it? Taste it? Smell it? The only way to manifest your dream is if you hold on to your vision of it for dear life. Otherwise, life's trials and tribulations will cause you to lose your willpower.

> *"Whoever's pain is bigger than his vision of his goal will lose his vision as he succumbs to the pain."*
> —Rav Ashlag

Get clear on what you want today. Now hold on!

Sticks and stones DO break our bones.

Kabbalistically, the power of words and speech is unimaginable. We hope to use that power wisely, which is perhaps one of the most difficult tasks we have to carry out.

Today, follow this wise suggestion:

> *"Spend more time watching what comes out of your mouth, instead of watching what goes in your mouth."*
> —Karen Berg

Today is the most important day of the year. Literally.

To be more correct, today is the last day of the kabbalistic year. It's the perfect opportunity to tie up any loose ends, offer any overdue apologies, and meditate on what you want in the coming year. Quite literally, we have a final few hours to wipe the slate clean before the curtain closes on this year's show, and the curtain rises on the year to come. So we'll spend the next few *Tune-Ups* focusing on how to take advantage of the seed-level energy available on the kabbalistic New Year.

If this information is news to you, do not fret; take a moment today and make two lists: One containing everything you want out of your life, and one containing everything you want in your life, whether it's already here or not. These two lists are going to be your guiding light for the coming days. As the saying goes, "If you don't know where you're going, how can you get there?"

September / October

Today is the most important day of the year. Again. It's the first day of the kabbalistic New Year. This means today is your birthday. The birthday of your soul, that is.

In the offices of the Upper Worlds, our cosmic files—the choices we could have made differently, the words we could have better chosen, the times we could have given more—are being reviewed. So in the Lower Worlds—i.e., Earth—you may be feeling heavy, lethargic, perhaps even tense and curt when dealing with others.

In the same way that the seed contains the tree and all the fruit it will bear, today is the seed of the year. Our task, therefore, is to behave today the way we'd like to see our behavior be all year round—despite the air of judgment from above. Plant as many positive seeds as you can this year.

How? Be happier, calmer, more secure, and more connected to the Light than you previously thought possible.

Today is the most important day of the year. Again.

Again?

The cosmic window is still open for us to write an open letter to the universe, asking for what we want, and letting go of what we don't.

But the truth is, every day is the most important day of the year, clichéd as this sounds. Why? Because today is the only day we can affect change. Today is the only day upon which we can reveal Light. Until tomorrow, that is.

So be your own vision of perfection. Don't let difficult people and challenging situations get to you. Share like today's the only day you'll have— because tomorrow, today will be gone, and with it, opportunities to reveal Light that will never come again. I'm not saying you should treat every day as though it were your last, but rather, treat every day as though it were your ONLY.

Now that we've planted positive seeds aplenty, we're given another gift from the universe to erase any dark marks from our past.

Our consciousness, words, and actions today— Monday if it's 2009, Saturday if it's 2010—are able to correct any darkness we revealed on all of the respective Mondays or Saturdays of the past year. Tomorrow, our consciousness, words, and actions can correct all of the negativity revealed on all of the Tuesdays or Sundays of the past year, and so on.

The important thing is to hold on to the idea that we can never lose hope, abandon ship, or give up, because the mercy of the Creator is infinite.

We always get a second chance, and a third, and a fourth ... and so on.

If only we could be as merciful with our loved ones.

When we began the kabbalistic year, we also began the month of Libra. And if you know Libras, you know that they have a gift for impartiality and non-judgment. Luckily for us non-Librans, we can borrow from this gift throughout this month.

Look at your own life and see where you're partial, biased, or perhaps a little too harsh on someone else. Try to see the other side of the coin. Feel the situation from the other person's perspective. And remember, your consciousness, words, and actions today can eliminate the darkness you revealed every Tuesday, if it's 2009, or Sunday, if it's 2010, of the year that just ended.

The month of Libra is ruled by the planet Venus, the planet of love and beauty—two things we don't see enough of in others. You know that person at the office who rubs you the wrong way? The cashier at the market who's always angry? The bully who pushed you around on the playground when you were a kid? They all have love and beauty within. Can you see it?

If you can't, it only means you're human. But we're here to go against our nature. So, look at those nasty, hateful people in your life and seek out the love and beauty. Doing so can help you correct the negativity from all of the Wednesdays, if it's 2009, or Mondays, if it's 2010, of the past year.

Want to take it even further? Spend time reminding people of their own love and beauty.

As you know, we are in the month of Libra. The beauty of Librans is that they see the good in everyone and every decision. But they also see the bad, and their ability to see both sides of the coin can sometimes immobilize them.

What decision are you wavering on? Don't let the energy of this week paralyze you. Make the decision and go with it 100 percent. Do this, and you'll be able to correct all the times you were immobilized in the Thursdays, if it's 2009, or Tuesdays, if it's 2010, of the past year.

Most people want to rest when they sleep. Unlike most people, the kabbalists always used sleep as a platform for spiritual work.

If you're going through challenges, did you know you can ask for solutions before you go to sleep, and quite often you'll get the answer in a dream, or even wake up with the answer?

If you are experiencing fears and anxiety, did you know you can ask for the strength to overcome them before you go to sleep, and perhaps even face your fears in your dreams, so that those mountains become molehills in real life?

Make plans to do some spiritual work tonight. And today, do what you can to transform the negativity you created every Friday, if it's 2009, or Wednesday, if it's 2010, of the past year.

What was, was.

If you are reading this, it means you've been given a second chance at working on your *tikkun* (soul's correction). You've been granted entry beyond the velvet ropes into this exclusive party called life.

Let's all commit to throwing away our security blankets of blame, anger, fear, self-doubt, self-destruction, self-beating, and hopelessness. And let's all commit to holding on to confidence, optimism, clarity, and consideration of the feelings of others.

What pain are you willing to release today?

What pleasure are you willing to embrace?

Doing this will clear away the cobwebs of uncertainty from all your past Saturdays, if it's 2009, or Thursdays, if it's 2010.

Don't worry, be happy.

The kabbalists teach that the innate quality of the Light is fulfillment and joy. There is no energy of sadness in the Creator's Light. Therefore, to connect to and draw Light we need to be similarly happy and blissful. That's why when we struggle to smile and celebrate, even in the face of difficulty, it feels so good.

Today, take an ax to the prison wall of your dark emotions. Let the Light in. And out. Doing so will spread joy on all the dismal Sundays, if it's 2009, or Fridays, if it's 2010, you experienced last year.

During the year, our consciousness is largely disconnected from our spiritual nature. We identify with our pain and chaotic thinking, unaware of the sparks of the Divine, which exist within. We live each day without access to our unlimited potential.

But today, on *Yom Kippur*, the spiritual atmosphere is unusually clear. We can open our minds and hearts to that little voice, and the answers we seek can become clearer to us.

Use the strength you've been given now to create a new destiny for yourself.

I've been exhausted all week. You?

It's understandable, considering we were just operated on—spiritually speaking. On *Rosh Hashanah*, the Light put our souls to sleep and removed the negativity attached to it. It's what the *Zohar* calls *dormita* (Aramaic for "slumber").

Now we're waking up from that procedure—and still a little groggy from the anesthesia. Plus, without the extra weight of our garbage, we are relearning how to live. That's why it feels like we are starting from scratch.

Go slow. The same way you would tell a friend who just went through something major, "Take it easy, you've been through a lot," cut yourself some slack. You don't have to conquer the world in a day. Test out your land legs. Take one step at a time.

There are moments when it becomes difficult for us to be lovingly truthful with others. Emotional blocks and fears can be paralyzing. It's easier to tell people what they want to hear. It's more comfortable to agree with someone, even when we disagree in our hearts.

Then again, it can be equally frightful to confront painful truths about our own selves—which compels our friends to tell us only what we want to hear.

Today, find the spiritual strength and courage to make those external and internal confrontations. If you need to speak difficult words of truth to your friend, ask the Light to awaken your compassion so that your words are born of love, not anger.

And if someone tells you something you're doing wrong, resist the impulse to fight back. Have the courage to be open to hearing it. You'll be grateful in the long run.

Balance is what we are all looking for, isn't it? A balanced bank account, balanced relationships, balance between work and play. Balance.

But most of us are imbalanced, aren't we? We take too much or give too little; we pig out for weeks, months, years on end, and then we go on crash diets expecting to be detoxed on the spot; we're cold and unemotional one minute, open and vulnerable the next. It's no wonder the world is so out of whack. In case you haven't learned this kabbalistic teaching yet, let me be the first to share it with you: Humanity is the center of the universe. As we act, so the world reacts.

Today, seek balance. Discover where you have swung too far to one side of the behavioral spectrum. Maybe you've been especially down and out lately, so find ways to pick yourself up and get out there with the people. Perhaps you've been everyone's doormat, so practice receiving for a change. Or maybe you're just perfect, so, hey, let me know your secret.

We know that we have been put on this planet to exercise our creative nature. If the nature of the Creator is pure sharing, then how pure is our sharing?

The kabbalists teach that today is one of the most powerful days of the year to give charity. And whether giving charity for you means donating your time, money, or love, give a little bit today. Make sure that at the end of the day you can say you made a difference in someone else's life.

Waiting for an external force to awaken our joy and happiness is precisely what keeps us lacking in joy and happiness. Happiness is a choice we make and must continue to make.

But what do you do when the conditions of your life aren't exactly joyful? Kabbalists recommend faking it 'til you make it. In other words, if you can't find the strength within, awaken it from without.

Smile. It feels good. When the muscles in your face contract, endorphins are released into your bloodstream, giving you that good feeling. Whether or not the smile is caused by the sight of your lover or because you're holding a pen in your mouth like a bone (try it for yourself), the body perceives that you are smiling, and it does its part.

Today starts the holiday of *Sukkot*, and the kabbalists explain that during this time of year, the energy of joy and happiness is ours for the taking, as long as we, ourselves, are in a happy state.

Today, be happy like it's your job.

It's easy for us to understand that we need to break the habit of allowing others to make us angry, sad, or depressed. But do we understand that neither should we let them make us happy?

Believe it or not most of the time our happiness is a reactive behavior. We let things or people be the cause of our happiness. But true happiness has no reason. It's a choice.

Think about one area in your life where you are waiting to receive something before you can be happy. Is it possible to be happy without it?

Do you recall the situation you focused on yesterday? Were you able to inject some happiness into it?

The *Zohar* explains that we see life backwards. We think we need the raise, soul mate, new car, or new body before we can be happy. But it's the opposite. Being happy now actually speeds up the process of achieving whatever it is we think our happiness depends on.

Continue to focus on that one area in your life where you are waiting to receive something before you can be happy. Be happy without it. And remember, practice makes perfect.

As we go through life, we wear three primary hats:
The Adult Hat takes care of business, the Parent Hat
takes care of others, and the Child Hat has fun.
It is important to have a healthy interchange of the
three.

What I notice is we tend to wear the first two hats
often, but the last one not so much. And yet, this is
perhaps the most important hat. As it's written,
*"So I command mirth ... because a man has no better
thing under the sun."*

Today, continue to find ways to be happy and silly.
Let go of the heaviness. The lighter you are, the
Lighter you will become.

Many great kabbalists have said that they achieved their greatness mainly through a constant state of joy.

It is important that we understand the logic of this spiritual law.

In the physical world, beings become close or separate through time and space. But spiritual entities become close or separate depending on their similarity of form. If two beings are similar in nature, then they are united spiritually. And if they are dissimilar in nature, then they are separate spiritually.

We know that the innate quality of the Light is fulfillment and joy. There is no energy of sadness in the Creator's Light. Therefore, to connect and draw the Light we need to be similarly joyful and happy. It is only when we are similar in this way that the Light can come to us and reveal even greater joy.

Rav Nachman of Breslov, 18th century Kabbalist once wrote:

> *Through joy, you can give renewed life to another person who is in a state of depression (or another fallen state). By approaching them with a happy face, you are able to give them renewed life.*

Smile. You never know whose life you might save.

We all fall back, spiritually speaking, from time to time. It's important to acknowledge where we messed up, but it's equally important to continue onward. Too many of us get down on ourselves and give up all together.

When he fell from the spiritual level he had attained, the great Kabbalist, Rav Nachman, said he did not feel depressed. He would just begin anew, as if he had never before stepped foot on the spiritual path.

He also said that through depression and sadness, a man can forget who and what he really is because his true essence is wrapped in so many layers of sadness. Therefore, it is necessary to fight to be in a state of joy—no matter how low you have sunk.

Restart your Kabbalah practice as if today were your first day. Forget about where you should or shouldn't be. Just smile, be happy, and know that your joy is a restart button on the game of your life.

How many kabbalists does it take to screw in a light bulb?

I don't know, either. I'm still working on that one. But I do know it's time to get happy!

The energy of the last month and a half has been sort of heavy. But that's about to change. The *Zohar* explains that a major benefit of the holiday of *Simchat Torah* (starting today) is the injection of pure, unadulterated joy into our lives.

Our plan today is simple: Be light, be silly, be goofy. Just be happy. Skip instead of walk. Dance with the kids. Listen to your favorite music.

The more you flow with happiness and joy, the more you're filling your tank with high octane for the year to come.

In my conversations with students over the years, and in my own life, what I have learned is that fears are often our greatest obstacles. They can burden and encumber existence to the point where we are fully preoccupied with them.

Fear is a bluff, which you must call—because on the other side of fear lie your dreams. If you run away from your fears, you are fleeing from the fulfillment of your own deepest longings and needs.

Today, continually ask yourself, "What am I afraid of?" The courage to conquer your fear is especially strong now. By proactively confronting your fears at the seed level, you will pull them out by the roots, and be done with them once and for all.

Imagine if you were called upon—right now—to justify your life before God. How would you feel?

Most people, quite understandably, would feel some degree of fear. But this is by no means a bad thing—as long as you understand your fear correctly.

Perhaps this fear will remind you of the things you should have done but didn't do. It might call to mind the too-numerous-to-count occasions when you acted selfishly. If you really had to explain your behavior to God, how important do you think desires for yourself alone would suddenly seem?

You can use today's energy to get in touch with the fear you might feel in honestly reviewing your life. By connecting with this energy, you can turn your fear into a motivating force for positive change in how you live, starting right now.

One of my favorite definitions of fear is:

False

Evidence

Appearing

Real

Fear is one big bluff; it's an imaginary brick wall we are meant to run through—head first. Think about it. Haven't some of your biggest achievements come as a result of pushing through your terror and anxiety?

Today, jump into the scary moments and know you'll be able to deal. This is where the real potential for growth is concealed.

In our hearts, we all know where we're going wrong. We all know how we're departing from our spiritual path. The problem is that we're either afraid of this knowledge or we don't want to do the work of correction that it requires.

If only we would open ourselves, listen, and not be afraid. As the 18th century Kabbalist, Rav Nachman of Breslov says: "The whole world is a thin bridge, and the most important thing is not to be afraid to cross it."

We must not be afraid of knowing what we have to do, because if we don't do it, we will have to come back to this world again and again.

And you don't want to have to go through puberty again, do you?

There is a wonderful story about a man who leaves this world and arrives at the pearly gates, where he is given a preview of Heaven and Hell. At first glance, both scenarios look the same: People sit around a huge pot of stew, holding wooden spoons with very long handles. When he looks closer at Hell, he sees emaciated people trying to feed themselves, but try as they might they're unable to get food into their mouths using the cumbersome spoons.

In Heaven, on the other hand, the people look healthy. The difference is that in Heaven they're feeding each other using their long spoons. They're sharing, because they understand that the only way they can eat is by taking care of one another. What is Hell? Hell is not having the ability to share with others.

Which scenario will you choose today?

A great sage once said:

> *"To questions there are answers, but to answers there are no answers."*

How many times do we ask spiritual questions when we already have the negative answer in mind? We ask questions rhetorically, as a way to put forth our opinions. This is not seeking truth.

Today, practice leaving your preconceived notions at the door when you ask questions about deeper spiritual truths. Open yourself up to objectively hearing the spiritual viewpoint.

Over the next few days, I'd like you to pay attention to reactive versus proactive words. For example, when you find yourself using the word "can't," try substituting the word "won't" and notice how your energy shifts from victim to Creator. "I can't do this" becomes far more empowering as "I won't do this." Now you're making a conscious choice.

Try being aware today and notice any shifts that occur for you.

I just want to tell you today that there are a lot of things you should be doing. You should be volunteering more. You should be taking more classes. You should be studying the *Zohar* more—a lot more.

How does it feel when you read this? Am I inspiring you? Or am I making you want to throw this book out the window?

Should is a terrible word. It creates resistance. It implies that we are not enough. And it's a word many of us use in our own inner dialogue. And that's one of the reasons we don't make good choices.

Should is never a good reason to connect to the Light.

Today, if you're feeling disconnected or a lack in your life, know that first of all, that's a good thing. Why? Because it's an OPPORTUNITY to use the tools of Kabbalah: To study more, to share more, to love more, to break a habit, to expand your Vessel.

Intention is the key here. Do it because you know it works. And do it with enthusiasm!

But please, don't do it because you should.

P.S. You should have a great day!

October / November

Are you one of those people who think things over and over and over before you act?

That's a Scorpio thing. And seeing as how we are in Scorpio, you might be "in your head" more this month than in others.

It's time to let go of the process of "cooking your thoughts," of constantly thinking things over. Get out of your head. You'll find all the reasons not to do something if you think it over too much.

Today, keep it simple. Do. Act. Move.

Kabbalah teaches us that all destruction—including war and physical violence, as well as all forms of natural disaster—occurs for just one reason: Man's hatred toward his fellow man.

Many of us here at The Kabbalah Centre want to change the world. But so many of us must change ourselves first. If we harbor hatred or animosity toward another person for any reason, valid or invalid, we bring destruction to our souls and to the world at large.

Today, visualize a person toward whom you feel animosity. Ask the Light to help you release these negative feelings, and to cleanse this hatred from your heart.

Remember, world peace begins with the person in the mirror. Peace expands when that person extends tolerance to his enemy.

Are you keeping score?

In relationships, at work, in life in general, we all do it. I can hear you thinking, "I am not a vindictive person." But how many times have you said to yourself, "I am not gonna let him get away with that!?"

We all do it to a certain extent—keeping a tally of who owes us and who we owe. This is unkabbalistic because it's not up to us to dole out rewards and punishments; it's up to the Light.

Today, if your buttons get pushed, remember, it's not your problem. You have more important things to think about. And it's not about, "He'll get his." It's about the fact that your time and energy are too valuable to waste being angry, hateful, and resentful. Next. Move on. The laws of Cause and Effect are at work, for all of us.

In a way, being a student of Kabbalah was easiest at the beginning. The new-found certainty, the miracles. But as daily existence extracts its toll, it becomes harder to recall those emotions of certitude, of excitement. It is difficult to evoke the feelings that motivated us during the first few steps of our spiritual path.

And that's just as our Opponent would have it.

Today, take breaks throughout the day and allow yourself to travel back to the person you were when you first found the wisdom of Kabbalah. Get back in touch with that appreciation, so that the truth of what you are doing may remain illuminated in your heart.

There is a story about a kabbalist who meets a fellow townsperson in the local apple orchard. Both the man and the kabbalist pick an apple from the same tree. The man looks at the kabbalist and says, "Amazing! We are so alike. Here you are, a great master of the spiritual world, and here I am, a simple man. Yet we both enjoy the same pleasures in life."

The kabbalist turns to him and says, "There is one thing that makes us different. You eat the apple because you are driven by your desire for the apple itself. I, on the other hand, eat the apple because I am driven by the Light that is concealed within the apple."

When enjoying the physical pleasures of life, remember the sparks of Light contained within. You'll enjoy yourself that much more.

Do you sometimes get this feeling that you just need to take a break and escape into the 1 Percent Reality? Scorpio is a high-pressure month, so don't feel guilty about doing what you need to do to recharge and realign yourself. If it's a manicure at the salon, or a shopping spree at the mall, or getting lost in a video game—do it.

Do kabbalists go to the movies or to concerts? Yes, we do. Because there is Light to be experienced in the pleasures of this world. And if these pleasures are invigorating us so we can serve as clearer channels for the Light, then it's all good.

A few students have e-mailed me, asking why I am promoting worldly pleasures.

There are other spiritual philosophies out there that say you should reject physicality—that it's bad to partake in the pleasures of the physical world. That's not at all what we're teaching at The Kabbalah Centre. If the *Zohar* makes one thing clear, it is that the world was created for the sake of benefiting its inhabitants.

We are not here to become beings of the *Desire to Share*; we are here to become beings of the *Desire to Receive for the Sake of Sharing*. Translation: We need to want more and get more in order to give more.

Every day, I read a new shocking statistic about the state of the world. Epic droughts, floods, epidemics, killer heat waves: The grim list goes on and on. We are facing a moment in time never before faced in all of history. It's no longer a matter of what we do today affecting tomorrow. It's what we don't do today that will determine whether or not there will even be a tomorrow.

Kabbalists and mystics have known for millennia what needs doing. Rav Ashlag knew it when he opened The Kabbalah Centre in Jerusalem in 1922. The *Zohar*—it's the only solution. It is the Noah's Ark of modern times. Without it, we are looking at dire consequences.

Every person reading these pages needs to take it upon him/herself to study the *Zohar* every day and to think of ways to distribute sets of *Zohars* to places in need: Bad neighborhoods in cities, emergency response teams, hospitals, prisons, homeless shelters, nuclear reactors, chemical plants....

If not now, when? If not us, who?

"You want to change, huh? OK. I'll send you a few tests to make sure you're serious."

I have a friend who made a commitment on *Rosh Hashanah* to stop being affected by what people say about him. Now he's being criticized more than ever! I keep telling him, "This is only a test, this is only a test."

Which commitments are you being tested on today?

Once upon a time, there was a little boy (or girl) who couldn't find a single solitary soul to give him love. No matter how many thousands of dollars he spent on therapy, no matter how many vision quests he went on, no matter how much he wore out his knees in prayer, he could not find one single solitary soul to give him the care and attention he craved.

One day, he found himself in despair and he decided to throw himself in the river. As he walked along the broken path to the bridge, he spotted a bum splayed out on the grass. On this bum's face was the biggest, broadest smile he had ever seen. "Maybe this bum has the solution to my dilemma," he thought.

The little boy (or girl) went up to the smiling bum and asked, "Mr. Bum, why can't I find someone to give me love?"

The bum retorted, "You need to give love before you can get love."

Are you this little boy (or girl)?

The *Zohar* says the eyes are like "pools of blessing." Through your eyes you can bring a flow of Light and love into anyone's life.

You've heard of the evil eye. This is the good eye.

Whenever you look at someone—especially a person you dislike—focus not on their physical self but rather on the Light of the Creator that is within. Doing this strengthens that person's connection to the Creator and helps them draw blessings.

Today, pick three people you don't like and practice giving them the good eye.

Oftentimes, when we say we love someone, we're actually referring to the way the person makes us feel. In a very real sense, our love for others is actually just an extension of our love for ourselves.

Yesterday, I was reading a parable that my brother Michael wrote:

> *A man walks into a restaurant. The waiter asks him what he would like. He responds that he loves fish. The fish is cooked and then cut up. The man then proceeds to swallow the fish. Is this love? Is this the way one treats someone he loves? This man does not love fish. He loves himself; he loves to satiate himself with fish.*

Think about this the next time you say, "I love you."

As children, we learn to "keep score." When someone hits us, we hit right back. And when we don't, we keep a running tally of punches owed.

As adults, we're no different. It's our nature to hold on to the slights.

The lesson for today is simple: Let it go. When you find yourself stuck in anger, practice thinking or saying, "Next. Next. Next." It's a powerful four-letter word ... and a lot nicer than some I can think of.

Money comes and money goes. We can always make more, but when time slips away, it's never coming back.

Kabbalah tells us that time is our most precious non-renewable natural resource. So we need to ask ourselves the following questions:

Am I being productive with my time, or am I just busy? Am I defining priorities and sticking to them? Or am I just doing … whatever?

This week, remember the words of King David: "Some live 70 years like one day … Some live one day like 70 years."

We all have our routines. Waking up at certain times, eating the same foods, sitting in the same place in class, going out with the same people. These are the things we do unconsciously.

This week is about the thrill of the first time. It's about breaking up our routines. It's about living each moment with consciousness.

Today, find one habit and change it. Do something you would never do. Get rid of this idea that there are certain things you don't do—"I never go to the theater. I never speak in public. I never…"

Doing what doesn't come naturally to us is a valuable restriction. It expands our Vessel and allows us to receive more than we currently have.

A kabbalistic legend describes a man who complained that he had no shoes until he saw a man with no feet. Look around and see where others have it worse than you. This will help you appreciate what you do have. Either we learn to appreciate things in our lives, or we will have to lose them to realize their value.

When you appreciate everything you have, when you are not worrying about why you don't have this, that or the other, then you have a chance to be truly fulfilled.

When you are busy focusing on what you don't have, you start losing appreciation, and when you lose appreciation, you can lose what you have.

Remember, the one who runs after what is not his is the one who loses what is.

Do you find yourself doing an awful lot of judging?

We are in the month of Scorpio, normally a time of tremendous judgment. But the kabbalists say we can also connect to a higher state of mind at this time, becoming more enlightened and aware. We have two choices: To be a part of the negativity, or to be spiritual and to overcome our judgmental nature.

Today, practice forgiving people. Believe me, there is always a good reason to criticize people, but it's just not worth the separation it creates. So just turn up the compassion, seek to understand the pain that motivates the ridiculous behavior of others, and be willing to let things slide a little. You'll be a lot happier in the end.

The *Zohar* talks about the circumcision of the heart. This sounds pretty strange without a deeper explanation. What it really means is that we have to work at removing hatred from our hearts. In fact, it says that a person who can't remove this hatred will never fully grasp what the study of Kabbalah is all about.

We all have difficult people in our lives, people whom we judge and dislike. But the fact is, a lot of troublesome people are only acting that way to cover up their deep insecurities. Hating a person prevents us from seeing the full person. In many cases, we may be just the person who can really help them, but we have to be open enough to see that.

Is there someone in your life whom you really can't stand? What pain might be driving them to be so exasperating?

Yesterday, I wrote about removing hatred from our hearts. One of the ways to do this is to rejoice at other people's happiness. No matter how spiritual we are, it can still be hard when someone close to us gets the very thing we want. Even if we say we're happy for them, that little voice inside of us says, "I wish it were me." That little pinch in our hearts is the seed of hatred.

When you feel the pinch, remind yourself that the Light sees you, too, and there's a reason you don't have what you want—yet. There is work still to be done.

Is there a friend of whom you're envious? Do you think you can find a way to be happy for them?

The kabbalists say any time we are in a confrontation with someone, it's not the first time we've locked horns with them. We've feuded together in a previous lifetime, and because we handled it poorly back then, a spark of our soul was trapped in that person.

When we say we "lost it" with someone, it turns out that we really did. We lost a part of our soul.

This is the deeper reason why we don't want to be reactive. The last thing we want to do is lose more of ourselves. Keep this in mind today as you interact with people.

It often amazes me how small we think. The Universe is constantly presenting us with a smorgasbord of lasting fulfillment, yet we tend to settle for scraps.

There is a story of a man who goes fishing. When he catches a fish, he holds it up against a ruler, and if it's bigger than the ruler, he throws it back. By the end of the day he has thrown back quite a few fish, and a fellow fisherman asks him why. He explains, "The pot I use to cook the fish is only 12 inches wide. I have no use for a bigger fish."

Life wants to give us everything, but when we're stuck with our small desires, it's as if we are throwing it all away.

Today, rethink what it is you want out of life. Expand your desires. Imagine that you can do or have anything, and allow yourself the courage to go for it.

Should I stay or should I go? The eternal question. Relationships. Jobs. Relocating. We've all spent time pausing at those doors. And how many times have we bailed only to look back in regret?

As we move forward in life, it's up to us to ask if this career, lover, home, is something worth fighting for. One question to ask is, "Am I giving up because of something small?" We can be with the perfect person, or have the perfect work situation, and give up because a little something happens that we probably won't remember a month or year down the line.

What doorway are you considering walking through today? Look back and ask yourself if you're hitting the road for the right reasons. Today is your opportunity to move forward on a new journey, or recommit yourself to the one you're on.

Positive action attracts positive energy, and each negative action attracts negative energy. It is these energies that either disrupt or develop our lives in many ways.

For example, oftentimes we don't understand what people are telling us, or vice versa. Miscommunication eventually leads to fights, arguments, and all too often, a whole lot of pain. It's as though there is an unseen interference pattern creating confusion and sending mixed signals; things go wrong for us, no matter what we do. Nothing seems to turn things around. These are simple examples of the influence of negative energies.

Pay attention to the words flowing from your mouth today, and the actions of your body. Ask yourself, "Is what I am about to do or say going to come back to hurt or help me?"

What does it mean to be holy?

It means being aware that the world is one complete whole and that we are connected to each other through the spark of the Creator that exists within us all. If we harm others, we are in fact harming ourselves. Mistreating another person is like sticking a finger into an electric socket. Yes, there are repercussions from our every word and deed. That is why sharing acts towards others are always in our best interest.

Turn this awareness on today. See the whole picture. In moments of conflict, treat others with respect and consideration. Feel what it's like to be holy.

Kabbalah teaches that sharing in a way that encourages others to become beings of sharing is the highest form of giving. And it has the biggest return.

> *"He who leads his friends to meritorious conduct benefits always from that conduct and the benefit never leaves him."*
> —The *Zohar*

Today, don't obsess too much over the details of your life. Instead, find ways to obsess over helping friends and strangers. You'll find the more you do this, the greater your blessings will be.

You're five years old. You and a bunch of neighborhood kids are playing hide-and-seek. You're it. 1, 2, 3, 4 … 10. You open your eyes—they're all standing there staring back at you.

Now, was that fun? No. For you to enjoy the game, all the kids must hide. The effort of finding them is what makes this game so much fun. The act of hiding is the mechanism that produces all the fun.

This is life, people. Our fulfillment eludes us because, otherwise, it wouldn't be so fulfilling. It's the hunt for love, money, health, friendships, and, ultimately, spiritual awakening that fuels our desire to live. If it was handed to us right off the bat, life would be dullsville.

Today, look at life as one big game of hide-and-seek. Enjoy the process of struggling, and know that if you are sweating, you're close to that which you seek.

What are your gifts? List them. Go ahead, take a moment and reflect on those qualities that make you special.

Got 'em? OK. How are you using them to benefit others? Kabbalah teaches that if we are using our talents for ourselves alone, we will eventually be hurt by these blessings. I don't mean to scare you, only to awaken you to the higher truth that you are a link in the chain of humanity and you have your part to do to uphold it.

Today, crack open your eyes a little wider. See the world around you and know that there are people living in darkness waiting for YOU to shine.

Real pain is a part of life. One of the things that happens is we become afraid of our pain and we avoid it. When we do this, we cause unnecessary suffering. When we are not willing to feel our pain, we also stop ourselves from feeling our pleasure and other feelings. It is like a faucet that is plugged up. In order for us to be in our greatness, we need to be able to feel our pain.

When we are not afraid of it, it flows—and passes. All feelings flow and pass. And even our pain can feel pleasurable because when we are flowing, we are alive.

Today, embrace whatever pain you may be experiencing—physical or emotional. Know that doing so will connect you to yourself more deeply; that is what this work is about.

There have been many moments in my life when I was frustrated with someone for not "getting it." Despite the agony of watching a friend or student or loved one suffer, I've had to remind myself of the kabbalistic principle: There is no coercion in spirituality.

We cannot force our opinions on others, even though we may think it is for the other person's benefit. We are not the policemen of the Creator. We can only share with an open heart and let the Light take care of the rest.

Is there someone that comes to mind when you read this? Who are you trying to coerce into believing, doing, saying what you think is the right thing?

My father's teacher, Rav Brandwein, always taught him not to judge a person by external appearance but to always search for that inner point within. He would often say, "Do not look at a container, but at what is in it."

We are always going to find something wrong with the people we live and work with—and especially those we love. Our job is to see past the misleading outer layers and to penetrate into the heart of what is good about the person.

Who do you need to apply this lesson to today?

November / December

Is there a situation in your life where you could really use a miracle?

Simply put, the Creator has given you everything you need to create the miracles you need. It is you who must activate the connection. Instead of waiting for nature to change, you need to change your nature.

But how?

Emulate the nature of the Light in your heart and in your actions.

And what is the true nature of the Light? It is to give and to share. The Light needs nothing. The Light has no need or intention to take. The Light only shares.

The more you become a sharing human being, the closer you come to the Light. And the stronger your power for miracles becomes.

Do you ever look up at the sky and say, "WOW!"?

I think most of us have had these moments, times when we looked at our children, or our bodies, or a tree, and were overcome with humility and gratitude. This awareness lifts us up, gives us insight, and allows us to live a purposeful life. (It is no coincidence that the word awareness begins with awe.)

Look up today. Be in awe. Feel the immensity of life and know that you are a perfect part of it.

It is a kabbalistic truth that no matter how difficult it is getting through to someone, if we come from a place of unconditional and unselfish love, we will eventually break down that person's resistance and connect with them. With true love, one can win the heart of any person.

I challenge you to focus your unconditional love on one person today with whom you've been struggling lately. Notice how difficult it is to put your judgments aside and just be compassionate and understanding.

As students of Kabbalah, one of the things we strive for is to awaken an inner realization that we cannot achieve anything of substance in this physical world without the help of the Creator (Light, God, Allah, the Divine, etc.). It's an understanding that nothing of value comes from us alone.

Yes, we have to work our butts off to make things happen, but we are not alone in this work. The Creator's hand can always be found.

Today, reach out and grab that hand. It may be just the thing you've been looking for.

Are you real? Do you put all your cards on the table, or do you hide behind a smiling mask, a fake version of yourself?

To a certain extent, we all do it to keep our true selves from getting hurt or feeling pain; unfortunately, it also keeps us from receiving the true
fulfillment that the Lightforce wants for us.

Our work now is to destroy that fake self. We do that by being vulnerable and willing to let people see our insecurities. It takes a strong person to be weak.

Open your heart today. Take a risk and speak your mind, even if it will cause you embarrassment. Especially if it will.

What do you do when you're standing in front of a thousand people waiting for you to talk, and you're just not feeling it? Or when your kids want to play with you after a grueling day at work and all you want to do is bury your head in the TV?

You train yourself to be excited. It doesn't come for free. The kabbalists teach that if you behave as if you are excited, in time you will feel excited. The key words here are in time. Practice makes perfect. Fake it 'til you make it.

The great kabbalists speak of reactive excitement. Something good is about to happen and we get excited. But if it turns out to be a false alarm, we get depressed. The whole idea is to find a happy medium in our emotional responses.

Today, when good things happen, think: "Wow. Great. Next." When bad things happen, think: "Wow. Great. Next."

"*I really want to work out this morning, but, ugh, I'm so tired and it's so cold and I have no clean socks and I need to replace the light bulbs and the gardenias need trimming and ... and ... I'll do it tomorrow ... tomorrow ... tomorrow."*
—Anonymous

We are not aware of just how negative a force laziness is in our lives. Laziness is anything that causes us to procrastinate, to do things slowly, and to avoid facing reality in the present. It comes from the gravity of body consciousness, which wants to keep things to itself. Our goal is to overrule this force and to connect to soul consciousness. We do this by resisting the downward pull of laziness, by running when we want to walk, by getting out of bed when we want to sleep just a few more minutes, etc.

Pick one thing you know you've been pushing off until tomorrow and do it today.

How's the family? Are you connecting with your siblings, folks, partner, kids, cousins? Are you treating them with kindness and tolerance? What about your friends, how is it with them?

When you can be kind to the people in your immediate circle, you will find it easier to be kind to all people. Today is a good day to create peace, to let go of harsh memories and old grudges, and to rediscover what it is you love about the ones you love.

Over the years, students come to me with their dilemmas, wanting to know what I think. Many times, I've answered by saying, "I don't have an opinion. What do you think?"

"You don't have an opinion?"

Of course I do. The Gemini in me has loads of opinions. But my opinions are not as important as your own.

We all get in the habit of running to our teachers, doctors, lawyers, parents, etc. for help, and it sucks our energy. We don't need to be running to people every time we have a question.

The Rav always taught me that asking questions and engaging life is how we connect. Knowledge is everything. Pursuing questions and figuring things out is how we connect our 1 Percent lives to the 99 Percent. Consciousness is the bridge.

When we sacrifice our free will for the sake of listening to others, we are severing our link to the spiritual side of life.

Today, I'm not telling you what I think you need to do. You figure it out.

We do things fearing they won't come out right. We doubt whether we can fulfill our desires. We have anxiety in the moment because we are disconnected from the final result.

But the second we create certainty, we are there.

What does certainty mean? It means tomorrow is already here and what I want to happen has already happened. I have found my soul mate, I have published my book, and my wounds have healed. It means knowing that as long as I am doing what I need to do, whether what I want happens tomorrow or in ten years, I know it will happen.

The space between now and then is illusionary. Remove the space. Be certain in everything you do.

How many miserable, cranky sourpusses do you meet in a day?

Practice sending them smiles. Get out of the habit of being offended by people or dismissing them. Forgive people on the spot and avoid analyzing them. When you feel the hatred welling up, dissolve it with a laugh. Don't be a hater. You've got the Light—use it.

The hardest of hearts is defenseless against warm words and a kind look.

Often times we wait for things to happen—around us, in our relationships, at our jobs, even within. One of the main reasons these things don't happen is because we don't demand change. We are content to go with the flow, to roll with the punches, to wait for life to change us.

Think about those areas in life that you won't change. We all have them; these are the situations we don't expect to change, so we don't work on them. And if you can't think of any, ask those around you:

"Where do you see that I've given up seeking change?"

You can change or you can be changed. Initiating the change is a lot less painful.

Did you take the trash out today? Imagine if you let it sit there, piling up to the sky, mildewed apple cores and dirty tissues everywhere. Yuck!

That's what it's like when you hold onto grudges. The resentment and shame stinks up our mind, creating a disconnect between our body and soul.

I think it's especially appropriate this time of year to talk about this. As we head home for the holidays, and all the old wounds are reopened and salted, there is a wonderful opportunity to take out the trash. We do this by forgiving.

Forgiving is letting go: Letting go of the memories that torment us, letting go of the people we once were, and letting go of the hatred we're holding in our hearts.

Forgive people for what they've done to you. And forgive yourself. You deserve it.

The following is a tale from the *Zohar* concerning forgiveness:

Near the city of Lod, a man sat on a ledge on a mountainside. He was weary from the road, so he slept. While he was sleeping, a snake came toward him. Then a lizard appeared and killed the snake. When the man woke, he saw the dead snake. He stood up and stepped off the ledge, and at that moment, the ledge fell to the valley below. He was saved. Had he risen a moment later, he would have fallen with it and been killed.

A spiritual master sitting nearby observing all of this comes to him and says, "What have you done that the Creator performed two miracles for you, saving you from the snake and from the ledge that fell? Those events did not happen without reason."

The man said, "In all my days, I forgave and made peace with any man who did evil by me. If I could not make peace with him, I did not sleep on my bed before forgiving him and all those who grieved me. I did not harbor hatred all that day for the harm anyone did me. Moreover, from that day on, I tried to do kindness by them."

Find time every night, before you go to sleep, to forgive people who have wronged you during the day. It's in your own best interest to let go of being right. It just might save your life.

While it is important for us to brush our teeth, eat three meals a day, and take care of our physical selves, it is just as important to take care of our souls.

Practically, this means reflecting on why we are here and thinking about the world we live in.

It's so easy to become completely immersed in our work, our possessions, and our physical lives. We tend to forget there's something bigger, something more substantial. Without remembering the meaning of our existence, the physical things become meaningless.

Today, think about why you are here. Think about why certain people are in your life. Think about what they can reveal to you.

Or simply consider why it's so hard to think about these things.

"Where is God?" people ask me.

Right here. God is in you. God is around you.

The only reason you might not be experiencing the full power of God's Light is because it is hidden behind a curtain. Being mean, hateful, disinterested, selfish, and the like puts up curtains. Fortunately, every time you overcome yourself and act in a tolerant, considerate, selfless manner, the curtain is drawn back. Keep in mind that the Light of God never changes. It remains constant. You have the free will to either remove the curtain and bring more Light into your world, or keep the curtain closed and increase the darkness.

Today, reveal the full intensity of the Light. Do something for someone for no good reason. Serve others before you serve yourself. Take yourself a little less seriously and others a little more so.

Kabbalah teaches that true happiness isn't a reaction to external events. You may have finally gotten the job you hoped for, or bought that car you longed for, or met the girl of your dreams. But before long, the joy dissipates.

Happiness is a force that emanates within us. When we bring our happiness to the world, the most ordinary experiences evoke delight. Suddenly, these experiences are no longer mundane. This is the nature of true appreciation.

Summon this force of happiness within you today. Smell the proverbial rose, spend a little extra time with the kids, do a jig for no good reason. Revel in the simple pleasures of life.

Some people don't ask for help from above because they don't think they know how. They feel foolish, inept.

The Maggid of Mezrich writes about this. He says that one who stumbles in prayer is "like a child who is very much loved by his parents. Even though he cannot speak well, his parents have great delight when he asks for something."

Today, feel certain in the fact that when you call out for help, your cries are being heard and appreciated.

You know those late-night infomercials begging you to "Act Fast?" That's actually pretty good spiritual advice.

We never know how much time we have on this Earth to do our spiritual work, so there is no time like the present, as they say. Whoever they are. We must constantly be on our toes, guarding against over-thinking and over-analyzing. And we must avoid getting our feet stuck in the mud.

Today, do things quickly. Don't get bogged down in any one thing, and if you do, repeat your mantra: "Next, next, next."

Beware the power of your words, say the kabbalists. You are the sole conductor of your fate, and what you say has the ability to change the course of your destiny. As my mother and teacher, Karen Berg, puts it:

> "With everything we do and say, there is a force that motivates. When we say things are rotten— that is what we expect, so they are. If we say things are good, things happen that way. We are the motivation for our own lives."

Today, be a positive motivation for your own life. Become addicted to optimism by constantly seeking out the Light amidst your darkness. It really works!

We tend to place more emphasis on our chaos, rather than our blessings, don't we?

We think about what we don't have, not what we do. We ruminate over who hates us, not who loves us. We go to bed at night thinking about who is fighting with us, rather than who supports us. This type of thinking only brings more of the same.

Today, flip the switch in your head. Allow yourself to see all the good that is within and without you. You'll know you're doing it right when the negative stuff starts to seem insignificant.

We all have an area in our lives where we have
trouble practicing restriction. For some, it is easy to
be spiritual in the home, but when it comes to
work, that is a different story. For others, having
tolerance for strangers is easy, but when it comes to
our family, we can't stop ourselves from reacting.

Today, focus on the area where you have the most
trouble being proactive. There is a lot of healthy
pressure now to change your nature, so if you make
the commitment to work on it, you are going to see
amazing miracles in your life.

An old Cherokee was teaching his young grandson one of life's most important lessons. He told the young boy the following parable: "There is a fight going on inside each of us. It is a terrible fight between two wolves. One wolf is evil. He is anger, rage, envy, regret, greed, arrogance, self-pity, resentment, lies, false pride, superiority, and ego. The second wolf is good. He is joy, peace, love, hope, serenity, humility, kindness, empathy, truth, compassion, and faith."

The grandson thought about this for a moment. Then he asked his grandfather, "Which wolf will win?"

The old Cherokee simply replied, "The one you feed."

Which are you feeding today?

Kabbalistically, we're in one of the most powerful times for creating miracles. That doesn't mean that miracles are supposed to happen now. It means now is the time to make them happen. So, for the next few days, we'll explore techniques for miracle-making, which you can find explained in greater detail in my book *God Does Not Create Miracles, You Do*.

Take note: Charity, by definition, is an act of giving or donating to those in need. Charity, within Kabbalah, is also the stuff that changes destiny. Giving, whether of your time, money, effort, wisdom, or possessions, is a powerful way to turn on the Light. The more difficult the action of sharing—in other words, the greater the stretch—the greater the revelation of Light, and therefore, the greater the miracle.

Be charitable today. But instead of doing it because of this suggestion, do it because you want to awaken the energy of miracles in your life for the entire year.

In a light bulb, the wattage is determined by the resistance of the filament. The greater the wattage, the greater the glow of the bulb.

In our lives, the degree to which we are connected to the Lightforce of the Creator is determined by the resistance we exert against our own natures. The greater the resistance, the greater the glow of the Lightforce in our lives!

Going out of your comfort zone is a great way to create miracles. Here are some "easy" ways to get uncomfortable:

- Choose challenge over the easy route.
- Don't seek anyone's approval or acknowledgment.
- Let go of the need to be right.
- Do whatever is contrary to what you normally do.

Be uncomfortable today. But rather than brace yourself for torture, brace yourself for miracles!

If an angel came to you in your dreams tonight, and told you that when you woke up, you'd experience a miracle, how would you behave the next day?

With excitement, anticipation, and joy, right?

The Kabbalists explain that it is precisely our excitement, anticipation, and joy that activate miracles in our lives. When we know they are coming, that paves the way for them. Our certainty that they are coming is actually what brings them to life!

Be excited today. Know that you have miracles heading your way.

The power of miracles is available to us at every moment.

There are many practical steps you can take to connect with this power. They all involve finding excitement and beauty in the permanent and lasting gifts of the Creator:

- Begin the day with gratitude.
- Realize that life itself is a miracle.
- Recognize the precision and wonder of nature.
- Seek the Light in every person you meet.
- Identify the Light in all things.

Exercise these five steps today and you will have the power of miracles on your side. Create the unthinkable—for yourself, for your loved ones, and for the world.

Creating a new reality of peace and serenity is the ultimate purpose of life. But there is a profound secret as to how to achieve this elusive goal.

Here it is: Every action you take to advance this cause for others brings you that much closer to a life of true fulfillment.

In other words, you will receive extraordinary blessings, protection, and joy in your life when you help miracles unfold in the life of another. That is the
secret. And that is the underlying power of sharing and caring.

I think you know what to do today.

A fish doesn't realize it's swimming around in water because it has no point of reference. But just take a fish out of its environment for a moment and then plop it back in the tank. The water will be exactly the same, but the fish's appreciation of it will be changed forever.

Today, think about how this metaphor might work in your life. Rise out of the water of your life, shift your paradigm, break the frame. Awaken to all invisible gifts and miracles flooding your life.

December / January

There is a fundamental principle in Kabbalah that we are the creators of our own reality. So, inasmuch as we must take responsibility for the obstacles and challenges we face, we must also be accountable for the miracles and wonders we create in our lives.

Therefore, part of the miracle formula is knowing that it starts with me. While the Lightforce of the Creator is the origin of all blessings in my life, I am the catalyst, the channel, the conduit through which those miracles come into fruition.

Be proactive today. Ask yourself, "Am I behaving in a way that creates and causes miracles?" If the answer is no, start now.

But whether the answer is yes or no, the power of miracles is ours until tonight. Follow the formula from the last few days, and happy miracle-making!

On this final day of the week of miracles, let's all dedicate time today to recognizing the abundant miracles in our lives. There are endless miracles:

- In the body's synchronicity.

- In the planets and stars.

- In the love between two people.

- And so much more!

As you enumerate the miracles in your life, you can also take a moment to ask for another miracle. Appreciation is key to opening yourself up for greater abundance in miracles and all areas of your life!

It's not the new things outside of yourself that you want in life. It's what you already have within that you want.

Most people go through life with a feeling of emptiness. But no number of new cars, boyfriends, partying, cappuccinos, or cheese Danish can fill this pit.

These are fun diversions, but do they last?

The only way to get to a place where you can experience this underlying fulfillment is by doing the spiritual work. When someone calls you to help them move a couch just when you're about to sit down to watch a ball game, or when your girlfriend is in a funk and all you want to do is have fun, or when you're down to your last 10 dollars and a friend needs to borrow five—these moments when you sacrifice your "What about me?" mentality is when you start experiencing true fulfillment.

Today, practice sacrificing your "What about me?" mentality.

Do you put your money where your mouth is?

The *Zohar* says that a person whose strength is in his words and not in his actions will always be caught in the world of extremes. That's why it is so important to walk the walk, and not just talk the talk. And we all do it, to an extent.

There is tremendous energy in our vows. When we make a promise and don't keep it, we create little voids of energy in our lives, which is why we are so often uncomfortable and dissatisfied.

Today, make sure what you put out there matches the truth of what you are doing. If there is any distance between the two, you are wasting your time, says the *Zohar*.

Focus on action today. What have you been procrastinating about? What are you "trying" to do? Don't try. Just do. You'll be much happier.

The days of looking to our leaders to solve our problems are over. This is not rhetoric. It is a fact. Look around you. Has violence disappeared? Is hatred a thing of the past? Have the hospitals been put out of business? No. And it is not the fault of our leaders.

Every single one of us needs to strive to be a leader. The reality is that whether we like it or not, we are the leaders.

Today, practice taking your leadership skills to the next level. Push yourself to speak up in one area where you normally would keep quiet.

Have you ever gone into the part of the bank where they keep the safety deposit boxes?

The way it works is there are two doors. You can't get into the second door unless you close the first one. This is the perfect metaphor for our lives. We are so often stuck in the past, either by holding on to limiting thoughts about ourselves or by licking old wounds. This prevents us from moving forward in relationships and every other area that is important to us.

Close the door on the past. You can certainly look back and learn from it, but don't focus on it. Every day is a new day. Be open to the magic of life. You never know what can happen today.

Kabbalah teaches that tornadoes, floods, earthquakes, and disease are born from the collective hatred that burns in our hearts. In truth, there is no such thing as a natural disaster. Human behavior and the human heart are the sole determining factors as to what occurs in our environment and what transpires between nations.

By cleansing the hatred in our own hearts, we can remedy all the world's problems at the level of their root cause.

Acknowledge someone toward whom you feel anger, envy, malice, total disgust, or any combination thereof. With all your might, drop those negative feelings like a load of wet laundry!

What are attachments? They're the things you don't choose to do, but do out of habit, from waking up at a certain time in the morning, to eating the same foods, to taking the same route to school or work every day. An attachment is sitting in the same place in class all the time, going out with the same people, going to the same restaurant.... You get the picture. They're things you do that create "safe" paths in your life.

Today, find an attachment and change it. Do something you would never do, stop behaving the same way—get out of yourself. Why? So you can receive more than you have in your life right now.

Thinking that you will be happy when a negative situation passes is faulty thinking. Being happy while it is negative—that's the secret.

Practice this today and see the miracles that occur.

The kabbalists teach that we each deserve to receive what we need.

Unfortunately, sometimes, due to different reasons —maybe a negative action or the like—we block the flow from the Creator to us. But sustenance still comes down into this world. It is given to another person who in reality does not own it, but rather is meant to hold it in trust. Eventually, he will give it back to its rightful owner.

This powerful lesson tells us that when we see or know of another person who is in need, we should share with them, but not with the consciousness that we are doing him a favor by giving him what is ours. Rather, we should realize that we are returning this abundance to its rightful owner.

One of the attributes of a kabbalist is the ability to challenge negative thoughts. It's not that wise men and women don't have them—no one can stop them—but they don't believe them. This is what makes sages wise.

What do you believe in today?

While we're engaged in an ongoing search to find and transform our ugly emotions into something beautiful, it's important to recognize that we're meant to have doubts, insecurities, and all the rest. They are a natural part of the transformative process.

I think once we learn a little Kabbalah, we freak out when we sense the doubt, anger, or fear bubbling up. We think we're doing something wrong. We are actually doing something right. Without mountains to climb, life would be one long, dull straightway.

Simply BE today. Accept yourself. Know that whatever plagues you also contains seeds of beauty which will soon bear fruit.

When we turn on the faucet to brush our teeth, does it ever occur to us that the water won't come out? Of course not. So why is it that when we turn the Light on in our lives, we doubt we are going to see the fruits of our efforts?

The answer is: If we want to see Light flow like water from a faucet, we must know it's going to flow. It's called certainty.

Be certain of what you do today. Allow the doubts to wash away and confidence to gush into every area of your life.

We tend to become too focused on the narrow agendas of our everyday lives. We need to learn to let the Light move us in the direction we really need to go. That direction may not be exactly what we expect, but in the long run, it's certain to be better.

Today, focus on being less focused. Look at your goals in life—at work, in relationships, in health, and in your own spiritual growth—and identify the limiting belief systems and narrow thought processes that may be inhibiting the Light from flowing into your life.

If a person's spiritual work and excitement are based on his feelings on a particular day, he is bound to fail. The kabbalists remind us we need to do the work even when we don't feel the "energy."

It's easy to be spiritual when you're pumped, but not so easy when you're flat. Yet, it's in the moments of blah that we can reveal the most Light.

Today, look for those points when you've had enough, when the last thing you want to do is share or connect to a spiritual tool. Remember the lesson above and push yourself. Sometimes it's that one extra step that makes all the difference—in your life and the life of another.

Besides reading these daily messages, are you studying other kabbalistic texts? Attending classes?

The kabbalists teach that it's important to study every day because it makes clearer the distinction between Light and dark. When we relax about our study, we slowly stop doing positive actions, and then we develop resentment toward others who study and reveal Light. We must watch ourselves, and not fall into this trap of laziness.

Have you fallen into this pattern? Pick up a book today or go to a class. Refresh yourself with the basics of Kabbalah, or bite into a difficult teaching and roll it around in your mind. Remind yourself of what Kabbalah is and why you began studying it in the first place.

Whether we want to believe it or not, at the end of the day, there are two forces in the world: Light and dark, or the Creator and the Opponent.

When things just land in our lap without any effort, we can know deep down that this smacks of the Opponent. When we take the easy route, when things come to us with little or no effort, we've stumbled upon the Opponent.

But when we work hard at something and experience obstacles—when there is a process— then know that this is the spiritual process at play.

Today, allow space for the process. When you are ready to give up on something because it's not coming right away, resist your desire to throw in the towel. This restriction will let the Light in.

You know that feeling when a relationship goes stale?

Kabbalistically, the likely reason is that you are receiving without sharing. This results in stagnation. Just as trapped water becomes stagnant, so does Light become stale when its flow is blocked. There is nothing wrong with receiving—we're supposed to receive—but if there is no sharing, then what we receive is limited and unfulfilling.

Today, share love. Share time. Share friendship. Just share. Put some love into everything you do. Whether it's giving kindness to the bus driver or your ex, come from a place of caring. This is what it means to truly live Kabbalah.

Kabbalah teaches the importance of praying for health and well-being all the time, even when nothing's wrong. Especially when nothing's wrong. We want to constantly feel like we are about to lose everything—even our lives. Why? To avoid complacency. To avoid getting stuck. To avoid thinking everything is OK. We're not here to have nice, quiet, undisturbed lives. We are here to be tested, to overcome, and to grow.

Today, contemplate this concept. Feel the immensity of life around and inside of you. Be grateful for the opportunity to be alive. Get in touch with your humility.

Saying you're sorry does not remove the other person's pain. Apologizing does not prevent you from having the same reaction again under different circumstances a week or two later. To correct a pain you caused another, you must eradicate the trait inside yourself that caused you to react in the first place.

In other words, recognize, admit, and acknowledge those ugly little traits that live within you, no matter how scary the prospect might be. Once you overcome the fear of acknowledging the lower part of yourself, go to the next phase, which is to work very hard at eliminating those traits from your nature.

Today, focus on one nasty trait inside yourself. You might not eliminate it in one sure shot, but you can start the elimination process by blasting it with the Light of awareness.

It's easy to be spiritual when we are lacking. But it's not so easy to maintain the flame once we've been satiated.

I have people coming to me all the time who are desperate to fix their difficulties. But once they get what they want, they don't have the same intensity of desire. As soon as the relationship is better, the money is back in the bank, or the health is restored, they're not as willing to do whatever it takes to connect. I am guilty of this as well.

Drawing energy from and maintaining an awareness of the Light is more important after we get what we want, because we do so without an agenda. It's a higher level of spiritual connection.

Recall a major prayer of yours that was answered. Do you remember the intense desire you had prior to getting what you wanted? Allow it to resurface today, and by doing so you will receive even more fulfillment in that area.

Spirituality is a bit like running up a down escalator. It's easy to fall behind.

We've all been there. Some of you are there right now, collapsed at the bottom stair, wondering if you'll ever get up again—let alone reach the top. Pushed down by doubts, laziness, anger, addiction, you may feel like it's over for you. "This spiritual stuff doesn't work for someone like me."

This spiritual stuff works for someone precisely like you. Remember, the dark side of your thoughts has its power. If you side with it, it'll hold you down—put its foot flat on your face. The only thing to do when you slip is to return immediately to the practices that sustain you and give you energy.

Which spiritual practice—sharing, studying, asking the Light for help, etc.—can you recommit to today? You don't need to sprint to the top. Just take one step. And the next. And the next. You'll get there eventually.

Every part of the body has a spiritual power. The eyes have the ability to help—or harm—other people.

Though it may seem superstitious to those who don't pursue spirituality, the kabbalists were quite clear when they taught that looking at others with greed and jealousy can bring actual harm. I'm sure you've heard of the evil eye by now.

Conversely, when we look kindly upon others, when we give them what is known as "the good eye," we can bring blessings to them.

Unfortunately, our insecurity and self-doubt cause us to give mostly the evil eye, especially to friends and loved ones. Do you deny this? I certainly don't. Today, in spite of the lack you may be experiencing and the fact that other people are better off than you, wish them well anyway. If you practice this— and make it part of your life—you will come to understand that this is the best way to fill the very lack you are currently feeling.

"*What* a *person does not do while he still has the power that the Creator has given him, he will not again have the opportunity of doing in the grave, for at that time he will no longer possess this power of choice and free will given to him.*"
—Rav Moshe Chaim Luzzato (the Ramchal),
    18th century Kabbalist

Windows of opportunity are open all around us. But for how long?

There is a joke about two shoe salesmen who travel to a third-world country in search of new business opportunities.

One man calls his wife the moment he lands, telling her, "Honey, I'm coming back home. There's no hope here. Nobody here is wearing shoes, so there's no one to sell to." He boards the next flight home.

The second man calls his wife and says, "Honey, you wouldn't believe what I found here. There is so much opportunity. No one here is wearing shoes. I can sell to the whole country!"

There's opportunity everywhere. When we have a consciousness of expecting the magic to happen, it will happen. We'll find the right people, we'll move in the right circles, and we'll bump into the right solutions. It all starts with that opening in the mind.

Open up today. Open wide!

Today, prioritize your life. Look at your day and see how much time you devote to what really counts: Serving others, sacrificing ego, and growing your connection to the Light. Stop pushing things off until tomorrow. There's no time like the present.

As spiritual people, we are always increasing our awareness of the signs and messages that come to us. However, at the same time, when we do see those signs and hear those messages, we, very often, shirk those opportunities and responsibilities with the thought that we'll always have another chance.

Thinking that another such window will open is erroneous. The reality is, we usually only have one chance to talk to someone, only one chance to do something, and we don't realize the value of these opportunities.

Each day brings us a once-in-a-lifetime chance. There may be specific people that we can touch today with whom tomorrow we will have no connection, no opening, and with whom yesterday there was no possibility.

Today, turn yourself towards the windows that open, no matter how subtle or quiet those opportunities may be.

It's rare to find someone who has genuine certainty about the Light. Most of us give the belief lip service, but we don't truly feel it. If we did, we wouldn't fight the obstacles in our path, or trash other people. We would be confident that difficult situations and people are sent to us for a benevolent reason.

Today, remember the bigger picture. All the things you see with your eyes come from the Light. Everything is a blessing.

Every painful experience in your life can be transformed into its exact opposite.

All of your suffering, your fears, and your hurts can be transformed into blessings and fulfillment. But you need to let go of the guilt and negative emotions you carry with you. This is not an easy thing to do. But everything that happens in your life is there to teach you something about growing as a person. Everything.

Today, choose a close friend or teacher to whom you can open up. Really open up. Once all your fears and emotions are out in the open, then, and only then, can you transform them into positive feelings.

One of the hardest things to remember is we are not the center of the universe. Contrary to how it feels sometimes, it's not all about us.

Today, observe how many of your daily actions and thoughts center on you. Practice getting out of your head and doing things purely for the sake of sharing with others. Don't think about the Light you will get, or not get, or maybe get. Just give some part of yourself to another human being and think only about their side of the transaction.

Happy Birthday!

Every day is a rebirth, a celebration of life. The mistakes of the past are gone and the worries of tomorrow have not yet arrived. Experience the power of your life, right now. Feel today as if it's your first.

January / February

A worm inside an apple has a limited view of the world. When it works its way out, it discovers a landscape far beyond what it imagined.

This is how we live. We have limited perspectives, and we don't see what we're missing. We only see what we are—we don't see what we can become.

Today, work your way outside your apple. What do you want to become next week, next month, next year? Where can you grow more, do more, be more? Dream big and you will be big.

Rav Zusha, the 18th century Polish Kabbalist, was lying on his deathbed surrounded by his students. They were surprised to see him crying and asked, "Why do you cry? You were almost as wise as Moses and as kind as Abraham."

He answered, "When I leave this world and appear before the Heavenly Court, they won't ask me, 'Zusha, why weren't you as smart as Moses or as good as Abraham?' They will ask, 'Zusha, why weren't you Zusha?'"

We each have a destiny to fulfill, one that involves discovering our unique powers and sharing them with the world. Have you discovered yours?

Today, ask yourself the simple question: "Where can I be doing more?"

"*Every soul must come to me, to Kotzk, for salvation, even if it is behind the Mountains of Darkness.... I could, if only I wanted, bring the dead back to life, but my purpose is to keep the living alive.*"
—Rav Menachem Mendel of Kotzk, the Kotzker Rebbe

The Kotzker Rebbe, an 18th century Kabbalist, is telling us that most of us are asleep!

Today, focus on an aspect of your life where you're not fully alive. Ask yourself what you could do to make the situation better? Take full responsibility, put it all on you, and ask yourself what you can do to make this situation come alive again.

As the *Zohar* explains, the greatest virtue a human being can have is humility.

And a key aspect of humility is being able to relate to everyone.

This is something that you must strive to incorporate into your life. As you fight to succeed in life, it might seem that it's the biggest and the best who win. But true success comes to someone who can put himself on the same level with whomever he is speaking. That's what humility is.

Today, think about the people you have the most trouble reaching. Be brutally honest and ask yourself, "Why? Why am I not reaching this person?" Ask yourself what transformation you must undergo to bring yourself to his or her level.

Speech is silver. Silence is gold. Remember this today when friends come to you for advice. By listening and resisting the urge to speak, you allow them the room to express themselves and discover the answers for themselves.

We spend our lives looking at our watches and counting the minutes until we can move to the next activity. We don't appreciate what we've got while we've got it.

A true kabbalist knows that every single minute counts, that this minute is presenting us with certain opportunities we will never again be presented. If we are focusing on what we didn't do yesterday or what we will do tomorrow, we are missing what we can do now.

This is worth repeating: You will never get this minute back again. Find the opportunity it's giving you and act on it.

Imagine two cups, one regular and one with a hole in the bottom. They're both receiving water. One cup can only receive a finite amount, whereas the other can receive endlessly.

The hole is what allows the cup to continue receiving. Without giving away the water, the cup will overflow and make a mess.

Are you getting it? If we wish to keep taking in, we need to keep giving out.

Apply this to your life. Think of a situation where you shared while receiving? How did it compare to simply receiving without sharing?

Life's obstacles are only a test. Kabbalists explain that whenever you hit a brick wall, if you push through it, you will find that most often, it is merely a soft curtain cleverly disguised to look like a brick wall—just to keep you from even trying to pass through!

It is a spiritual law of the Universe that the fulfillment you are searching for is always concealed before it is revealed. It's up to you to strive to uncover this fulfillment.

Find a nice, thick brick wall to tear down today.

Remember what it was like being a kid?
Constantly being told what to do, to think, to say.
We swore we'd never be controlled again.

Now that we are grown up, doing our own thing,
we are under the illusion that we are no longer
controlled by external forces. The truth is, we still
are. Every time we allow our buttons to be pushed
by others, each moment we let a situation that looks
negative freak us out, we are being controlled by
outside causes.

Becoming aware is what allows us—once and for
all—to take control over our lives. Mindfulness is
everything in Kabbalah.

Be present today. Notice your reactions to the
people in your life. How often are you allowing
what others say or think to hinder you?

Being spiritual doesn't mean stuffing our feelings.

Yes, Kabbalah teaches us to be non-reactive. But that doesn't mean we must be non-responsive. People's actions are going to make us churn inside, and get our minds thinking nasty thoughts. The goal is to resist the urge that comes from the ego, and to respond from a place of Light.

Today, as your buttons get pushed and your wounds salted, practice responding Lightly.

Maintaining a spiritual focus requires constant refocus. As with a camera, our spiritual instincts become blurred during the process.

That is why many a kabbalist strived not to be depressed when they fell from the spiritual level they had reached. They would simply start over, as if it were their first step on the path.

Give yourself a break. If you haven't exactly been Mr. or Ms. Loving Kindness lately, begin anew today. Find little ways to show tolerance, love, compassion, or any of your higher qualities.

I was thinking about something my mother and teacher, Karen Berg, said:

"We are never judged by the big things we do, but by the kindness that we forget to share."

Who are you forgetting to be kind to today?

When people are hostile towards us, it's usually because they're crying out for help. It doesn't seem like it, but nothing is ever what it seems, is it?

Do the unexpected today. If you're locking horns with someone, look them in the eye and ask if you can help. They'll be expecting you to hate, not to care.

Be real about it. Inquire about what is going on. If you are genuine, you just might find something out. And then you'll notice a shift in your own thinking from "How can I destroy this guy?" to "How can I help?"

Sometimes it feels like we are judging machines. We spend so much time stuck indoors, calculating, analyzing both ourselves and others. Too much judgment keeps us from acting.

Get out of your head today! Look out the windows of your eyes, ears, nostrils and mouth. Take in the infinite sensory experiences happening all the time.

Keep yourself moving. Analysis is paralysis.

When will there be peace in the world?

If we go the extra mile to bring peace between each other, then our neighbors will want to be at peace with us. If we are not at peace with our friends, with our brothers and sisters, how can we think about being happy with the rest of the nations of the world?

Today, create peace with yourself and others, and among other people. Do everything you can to transform from being a receiving person to a giving one.

Some people quit studying Kabbalah when they don't see miracles materializing right away. What they don't understand is if they don't strike gold after two or three digs, they mustn't blame the earth. They must dig deeper.

Dig deeper today. Share until it hurts (or helps). Dust off those Kabbalah books from the shelf and give them another read. Study the *Zohar*. The treasure is there; you only need to work to reach it. And work hard.

One of my mother, Karen Berg's, favorite mantras is:

"Next. Next. Next."

As you expand your Vessel (desire), there are going to be challenges and discomforts. You're going to get rejected and bruised. Your job is to grab your lessons and go. Next. Too many of us get unnecessarily weighed down by troubled pasts, broken relationships, and childhood traumas.

When a butterfly emerges from its cocoon, does it bring the cocoon with it? Next.

Today, let the rejection in. Feel the burn. Break the shells surrounding your soul. And remember to let go of them once they break. Next!

Doubt creeps in the moment we lose our focus on our original intention.

Think of it in terms of relationships. You could be so happy, you're with your soul mate, life is wonderful. Hugs and kisses, and all that. Then he or she does something you don't like and you forget. You forget how she helps you through the darkness. You forget how she loves you even when you don't love yourself. You forget. And then doubt creeps in. One moment you have every reason to be in the relationship, the next you find all the reasons not to be.

It's all about doubt. Why? Because you forget why you were in the relationship in the first place.

Today is your chance to remember. Remind yourself of what you receive from your significant relationships. Connect to the seed of goodness and cast out the doubt.

Everyone in our life—one way or another—comes to help us in our correction process. Even the people who may hate us: Ex-husbands, disgruntled employees, downstairs neighbors, former friends. Every person in our life is here to awaken another part of our correction.

It doesn't mean we aren't going to react. We can't always expect to thank someone who slaps or slanders us. But in the bigger picture, if we look at ourselves from afar, we can see that everyone in our life is here to teach us.

Today, as you deal with unpleasant people—especially the ones taking a big bite out of you—say a silent "thank you." Know they are there to open something for you in your corrective process.

Sarcasm, jitters, cigarettes, drugs, candy, tantrums, the silent treatment, yawning, yelling, obsessing, cheating—these are some of the wonderful ways we ruuuuuuuuuuuuuuuuuuuuuuuuuuuuuuuuuuuuuuuuuuuuu uuuuuuuuuun from our pain.

As I wrote recently, the only way to get to Heaven is to go through Hell. It means continuing to disengage from the delusion of the ego by facing the pain head on—whatever your pain may be. It's the only way to find reality underneath.

In what way are you hiding from reality?

A great kabbalist once asked his students, "Where does God live?" They quickly answered, "God lives everywhere." But he would not accept their answer. He taught them, "God lives wherever man lets God in."

God created you so God could share with you. In other words, you are loved. All you need to do is open your heart, think about others, and do the uncomfortable. That's not too much to ask, is it? I know, I know, it's easier said than done.

Today, give out some love—and let the Light in.

I think one of the things that I love most about Kabbalah is that it teaches us that it's not enough to fulfill ourselves. True fulfillment occurs only when we fulfill the needs of others.

Rav Menachem Mendel of Kotzk, the great 18th century Kabbalist, knew the wily ways of the ego all too well. He was known for his blistering brilliance and his unwillingness to play the ego games most of us play (that's probably why his schoolmates called him "Black Mendel").

He wrote: "Some people wear their faith like an overcoat. It only warms them, but does not benefit others at all. But some light a fire and also warm others."

It's a wonderful reminder of how wrapped up we can get in our "spiritual growth." Many of us are deluding ourselves in thinking that we are transforming. Without lighting fires for others, there can be no spiritual growth. I challenge you today to look at your life and see how much time you are devoting to warming the lives of others.

The last place you'd find most people is where they are. Most of us spend our lives thinking about what's next, who we're going to meet, who we're going to be when we get married, or whether we'll be skinny, rich, or famous. You know, life is what happens while we're busy making other plans.

But life doesn't happen in the future—or the past. It happens right here, right now. That's why it's important to start each day wherever you are.

Today, shake yourself free of any expectation. Encourage yourself to be fully in the moment—to enjoy your transformations and to seek out new obstacles. Sink your teeth into the endless dessert that life is serving up every moment of the day.

The *Zohar* teaches there are three ways to learn our lessons in life:

- Concealed: The voice within awakens us (least painful).

- Friends: A friend awakens us (moderately painful).

- Revealed: An external situation awakens us (most painful).

When a person is not hearing the warning voice from within, it is the responsibility of a friend to positively confront them with love. This prevents the other person from having to learn the lesson in a more painful manner.

We need to be able to awaken others—from a place of caring—and we need to be able to withstand it when they awaken us.

Focus on one of your close relationships today and find one area where the person needs awakening. The question to ask before saying a single word is: "Do I really want the other person to grow ... or is this area just bothering me?"

Every difficult situation is sent our way to help us to grow. Too bad we push the uncomfortable away.

Let's say you're in severe financial difficulty. God comes to you and says you will receive a million dollars every time someone hurts or angers you— provided you completely let go of any reactive feelings. Simply put, you cannot take anything personally. You have to let it go!

What would be on your mind all day? You'd be praying for God to send you people to hurt you. You'd wake up every morning searching out difficult relationships and offensive people!

The fact is, when you live your life with this in mind, you receive something more valuable than a million dollars. You receive the Light, which already includes financial sustenance, rejuvenation, well-being, happiness, and peace of mind.

Today, embrace the uncomfortable. Look for the silver dollar in every dark cloud.

Stop interrupting me!

Seriously, are we not all guilty of poor listening from time to time? The kabbalists teach us that life is all about connecting with others. How can we really love and understand others if we are not listening to them? If we continually cut people off, we stop them from connecting with us.

Today, simply notice how hard it is not to interrupt.

While the kabbalists are all about treating everyone with human dignity, it doesn't mean we have to live in dysfunctional relationships. Sometimes, we do need to show people the door, albeit politely.

How can we be sure we are doing the right thing? Maybe saying goodbye is just shirking responsibility. How do we know?

Write down all the attributes of the person. Would you feel a void if that person was no longer in your life? Is this a situation you can change; can you help the other person to change?

If the answer is yes, and it is worth the effort, then go for it. Tackle the challenge. Otherwise, maybe it's time to have that talk.

Rav Ashlag taught that being around people with bigger desires for growth, transformation, and Light helps us to reach beyond our own limited desires.

Today is the perfect day to look at the types of people you surround yourself with. Are they helping your growth? Or hindering it? What actions can you take to surround yourself with positive, spiritual people?

Good and bad traits are two sides of the same coin.

Our job is to constantly be flipping the coin to heads. Let's say you're jealous. What's the flip side of envy? Having a big desire. Nothing wrong with that, in fact, the more desire the better, provided it's channeled down the right route.

Today, think about those parts of yourself you're not too proud of. Can you see the Lighter side? Really look for it because the moment you recognize it is the moment you can sift out the bad stuff.

A student once approached a wise sage who was extremely well-versed in the spiritual doctrines and mystical arts. The student asked the master to teach him all the sublime secrets of life, to explain all the magnificent mysteries of the cosmos—all in the time it takes to remain balanced on one leg.

The great sage carefully considered this request. He then smiled warmly and replied, "Love your neighbor as yourself. All the rest is commentary. Now, go and learn."

Now, go and learn.

February / March

I have no great mysteries to reveal today. All I want to say is: Smile. That's it. Smile. Laugh. Be happy.

Let's say you're not fulfilled in your relationship or lack thereof, or your health is not what it could be, or your job is a drag—I say smile, anyway.

If there's one thing the *Zohar* teaches us, it's this: *Joy is the greatest healer.*

Laughing in the face of hardship arouses immediate and direct pleasure. Laughing ensures that hardships pass quickly and easily. Laughing allows us to regain control of our own happiness, rather than surrendering to external circumstances.

Heard any good jokes lately?

The forces of negativity exist in the world to give you a choice between chaos and the Light. The most powerful weapon of these forces is doubt.

You are tempted to lose trust in the power of the Light. You are encouraged to settle for a life in which uncertainty is a constant presence.

An important step for moving from the realm of doubt into the realm of certainty involves Thinking Big.

Certainty depends on enlarging your awareness and your aspirations.

Certainty begins to take hold when you realize that the everyday world is only a tiny fraction of the true reality.

Ego is not always bad. As with everything, there is a positive side to it. Knowing you are capable and talented is essential if you want to make a difference in this world. If my parents didn't appreciate their power to reach people, well, who knows where we'd all be today?

But the trap most of us fall into is we think the brilliant ideas are our own. They're not. The effort is ours, and the channeling is ours, but the content is pure Light.

Food provides us with the physical strength to do our work, but eating is also a major spiritual responsibility. The sages explain that there is a soul within every piece of food. The souls can't do anything by themselves, but once the food becomes part of us, our actions also become connected to the food's soul. A positive action on our part, then, becomes connected to the soul in the food as well, and we help to elevate that soul.

Keep an awareness of this responsibility when eating today. Chew your food longer and slower than usual. Ask yourself what positive actions you want this food to help you accomplish this week.

I once heard something very beautiful and I would like to repeat it: Happiness is like a butterfly; when you try to catch it, it runs away. But when you turn and busy yourself with other things, it comes and sits lightly on your shoulder.

This is a good lesson. When you really want to feel content, busy yourself with helping others, and in that way, your life will be enriched far deeper than you can ever guess.

A nation at war is merely the effect of a spiritual darkness born of intolerance among individuals who comprise that nation. Friction and disunity among people is the source of this conflict.

Peace begins with the individual in the mirror. Peace is kept when that individual extends tolerance to his neighbor.

Get along today. The world depends on it.

If we allow our ego to convince us that we are a somebody, then spiritually we are a nobody. If we resist our ego and consider ourselves a nobody, then we most definitely are somebody.

Today, focus on the qualities of humility, humbleness, and modesty. Be aware of the interdependence among all human beings, and of the vital importance of becoming a team player in the game of life.

Sometimes we forget to believe in ourselves and we need our friends and lovers to remind us of what makes us special. We can grow out of our darkest holes by being showered with love and kind words.

You are not going to believe this, but someone passed by me—just this second—with a T-shirt reading "Hugs Not Drugs." Talk about messages from the Light. That's exactly the point. Why do we do drugs and take part in other destructive behaviors? We don't love ourselves. And that's the gift our parents, children, friends, and teachers can give us. They can remind us we are loved.

As John Lennon sang, *"Love is all we need."*

Today, burn through layers of a loved one's doubt and shame with four simple words: I believe in you.

Recently, I was reading about an enormous island of trash twice the size of Texas floating in the Pacific Ocean somewhere between San Francisco and Hawaii. The so-called Great Pacific Garbage Patch has been growing since the 1950s, and is 80 percent plastic and weighs more than 3.5 million tons.

The alarming lesson here is just because our garbage is no longer in front of our face, it doesn't mean it's gone.

And so it is with our issues. Just because we broke up with the girl who was annoying us doesn't mean our lack of tolerance is gone. Just because we drink and smoke doesn't mean our loneliness or depression is gone. Just because we boss our employees or children or spouse around doesn't mean our feelings of inadequacy are gone.

Today, spot the ways in which you push your garbage away. Clean up your junk—correct it, rather. Feel the discomfort and deal with the problem, head on. This is the best way to clean up the polluted waters of your life.

A student wrote to me this week, "For the last two months, I've been restricting in this one area of my life. But I'm still not seeing any changes."

While restriction is a great start, the student is forgetting to throw away the calculations. When we sit and wait for the result, it will never come.

A student goes to his teacher and says, "Teacher, no one loves me." The teacher says, "Run away from love and love will run after you." Easy enough. Two weeks later, the student returns and says, "It's not working. I'm running, but it's not running after me." The teacher says, "You are running, but you keep looking over your shoulder to see how far back it is."

Today, don't look back and don't look ahead. Just look at the spiritual task in front of you. Submit to the process and let go of the need for results.

I didn't mean to hurt you. Honest, I didn't. Can you forgive me?

Forgiveness is much needed in this life. The Creator forgives us every day for the silly things we do to others and ourselves. Why is it so hard to extend that forgiveness to other people?

I guess I know the answer to that. I've held grudges before, shut myself down, and stuffed my emotions. But, sooner or later, it blew up and I only felt worse, and less connected.

Beneath all the garbage, we are all good inside. It's only our ego and our behavior that are less than choice. One of our human weaknesses is we can't differentiate the person from the behavior.

Today, take time to talk to your friends and lovers and let them know what's going on inside. Communication is everything. Letting it well up inside isn't healthy. We become stagnant, stale, sad—and we run the risk of throwing it all away. Express what you're feeling, listen to what someone else is feeling, and forgive. Remember the love. Forgive the nonsense. We are all perfectly imperfect. Forgive.

The arrows that pierce you the most are the ones released from your own bow. Self-doubt and self-hatred—these are your biggest obstacles in life.

Learning to love yourself is essential if you want to be somebody in this life. And that's not just self-help talk, either. The Light of the Creator is within you. It is your true essence. Recognizing this is not arrogant or egotistical. On the contrary, not recognizing your inner light is a denial of the Creator's Light.

Today, cast yourself in a favorable Light. See yourself as the good person you truly are.

My father and teacher, the Rav, gave an incredible lecture to the community in Los Angeles. As always, many inspiring things were said, but one of the most inspiring comments was this:

> *"I had the merit of having a teacher that was fully knowledgeable, fully understood, and lived the life of a kabbalist. And lived it! That is not easy. That is, in fact, one of the most difficult aspects of my whole involvement with Kabbalah."*

What the Rav meant by "lived the life of a kabbalist," as he explained later in the lecture, is the idea that at all times, one must follow the cardinal rule of "Love your neighbor as yourself."

I ask you today, whether you are a long-time student or this is just the beginning of your journey, are you treating people the way you wish to be treated? Are you extending the courtesy of allowing people to be themselves without trying to change or fix them? Are you genuinely loving people?

This is a question we want to continually ask ourselves as we face our friends, our colleagues, our family—and, most importantly, those whom we find difficult to tolerate. This is the test of a true kabbalist.

When you start something new, it's only natural to feel excitement and passion. But like all of us, you start to doubt yourself.

> *"Remember what Amalek did to you on the way*
> *as you were coming out of Egypt."*
> —Deuteronomy 25:17

Kabbalistically, *Amalek* is a code word for doubt. It's thoughts like, "This will never work," "I'm not smart enough, why am I wasting my time," or whatever destructive dialogue runs through your mind.

Today, find those areas in your life where your excitement has cooled down. Remind yourself, it's not you talking, it's Amalek. The passion was real, and still is. Fight the doubt, and return to your original intentions.

That's how you turn the heat back on.

What destroys our happiness?

Envy. Being busy with desiring what other people have. This takes our focus away from appreciating all the wonderful things we, ourselves, have, leading to a sense of lack and unhappiness.

Today, learn appreciation by imagining what life would be like if the things, people, qualities, abilities you do have were taken away. Every time you find yourself fixated on the glittering lives in the pages of *People* magazine, or the shiny new toys your neighbor has, bring your focus back to your life. Come back home to yourself, to your life, and look around. What if these things weren't here tomorrow? How much would you miss them?

Rav Akiva, the teacher of Rav Shimon bar Yochai (author of the holy *Zohar*), was forty years old when he began to study the secrets of Kabbalah. He did not think he could do it after having lived such a different way of life all those years.

One day, he passed a stream and noticed a hole inside a rock caused by years of tiny drops of water. Rachel, his wife, encouraged him, "If it takes the rock many years to form a hole, it is a sign that it must take all of us time to change and let the Light in," she explained.

Imagine if he hadn't learned this lesson. Imagine the world without the teachings of Rav Shimon. Imagine the world without the Light of the *Zohar*. There'd be nothing to imagine, as this world would cease to exist.

Four words for you today: YOU CAN DO IT!

The goal of spirituality is to love your neighbor as yourself, right? That means if you're doing your job right, you love yourself.

Do you? Do you appreciate who you are and what you bring to the table? Do you feel adequate, competent, enough? If I asked you to make two lists, one of the things you hate about yourself, the other of the things you love about yourself, which would be longer?

I meet so many people who downright hate themselves and it pains me to see it. Even the worst among us have so much love and joy and sweetness to reveal. All it takes is learning to accept ourselves a little more, each day.

Today, get in the mode of being good to yourself. If you mess up, be gentle; talk to yourself in a soothing, kind voice. "It's OK. I am learning. I am getting better every day." The more we open our heart for ourselves, the more we can open it for others.

If you want to know what your life looks like, look at your thoughts. If you don't like what you see, then change the way you think about life.

Most of us are stuck in thoughts of fear, disappointment, anger, and regret. We recycle the same stinkin' thinkin' again and again and again. It feels so suffocating after a while, doesn't it?

Today, air your mind out. Open the window and let the breeze come through. Stick your head out. See those people over there? They are potential new friends. Go talk to them. See that "Help Wanted" sign? That's your new career. Walk in and submit an application.

Allow new, happy, optimistic thoughts to take over for a change.

We are all looking for the same thing: To connect with our soul in order to receive guidance and deep, meaningful messages. There are a lot of Kabbalah books out there on the market these days that promise you this. Some are good, others not so good. Most of them require a PhD in Kabbalah just to understand them.

Do you want to know a profoundly simple way to receive guidance from your soul, every day and every night? Here it is. Ask yourself: "Am I taking or giving right now?"

When you take a deep breath in, you feel pressure in your lungs that forces you to breathe out. But in life, we don't see how much we are taking and how much that blocks our connection to our souls. You'd be amazed how much clarity you can gain by restricting your taking and expanding your giving.

Do it today. Ask yourself, over and over, "Am I taking or giving? Am I taking or giving? Am I taking or giving?" You'll get the hang of it.

In speaking with someone, how do you know if you are speaking from your ego or your soul?

Is your mind calculating ways to hurt or get something from the person, or are you in the flow of the moment and thinking about how you can help and share with the person in front of you?

Check in today. When you are negotiating with colleagues, making dinner plans with your girlfriend, or just paying for your Frappuccino, check in and see where your head is at. Be honest and check in with your true intention to determine who's talking—your soul or your ego.

I can't tell you how many e-mails I get from students who think I am mad at them because I didn't respond to an e-mail they sent or return their glance at an event. I, myself, experience this, too, especially when someone answers me curtly—or not at all. What's his problem?

Exactly. What's his problem? Or her problem? We've all got troubles, and most of the time, the reason we are reticent, reactive, or removed is because we are going through something and need some space or some understanding. Just as we want others to understand that we have issues and cannot always be on our best behavior, it's wise to remember that others want that, too.

Today, when you find yourself getting ticked off by someone because they ignored or snapped at you, remind yourself, "This is not about me."

My brother, Michael, was addressing students in Los Angeles one time about the importance of appreciation. He repeated something my father taught us growing up: *"The moment appreciation is lost, the relationship is lost."*

Appreciation is especially relevant now, when the energy of doubts is at its strongest. The lesson to remember is: Our connection to others, ourselves, and, ultimately, to the Light of the Creator begins and ends with appreciation.

This is something you know. I simply wish to remind you of the vital importance of constantly fighting for appreciation. And make no mistake, it's a fight. A battle. A war. It's easy to erupt in anger and indignation, but far more difficult to fight the internal battle against ego, or jealousy, or insecurity, or resentment, or doubt, or ... you fill in the rest.

Who are the people in your life whom you've begun to take for granted? The best way to get that thankfulness back is to imagine what life would be like without them.

Wʜat we hear depends largely on how we listen. When we listen with our desire tuned in to the frequency of sharing, we can find delight and wisdom in any sound. My father and teacher, the Rav, writes:

> This is why it is possible for a wise man to listen to the words of a fool and hear wisdom while another man, who may possess a genius IQ but who is motivated only by the Desire to Receive for the Self Alone [ego], may sit for years at the feet of an intellectual or spiritual master and not understand a single word.

Pay attention to where your head is at today. When your wife is telling you about her stressful day, or your client is complaining about a misplaced order, or your child is asking for the tenth time why the sky is blue, notice where your desire is. Do you have the person's best interests in mind, or is your mind elsewhere?

There is a story about a woman who decides she wants to find God. She gives up her worldly possessions, flies to India, climbs the highest mountain, and sets about praying and meditating. She calls out to God, "Where are you?!" and God answers, "I'm down here with the people!"

We don't all have to take a vow of poverty and live in an ashram to connect to our Creator. We need only to connect to others to find what we're looking for.

Today, devote yourself to three people. Find it in your heart to make them feel better, to meet their needs, and to motivate them to become more involved in their lives.

Kabbalists have long known that our thoughts shape what we perceive as reality every bit as much as reality shapes our thoughts. We are more than mere observers of reality—we are creators.

It is we who produce and direct our own movie— the same movie in which we ourselves are the stars.

What movie are you creating? Is it a love story? A comedy? A horror show?

Sometimes, it seems that when you read a Kabbalah book, or listen to a lecture, the same things are repeated. On *Pesach*, we talk about removing the ego; on *Chanukah*, we talk about tapping into miracles; on *Shabbat Pinchas*, we talk about healing. But recently I realized that it's not the wisdom that stays the same; it's we who stay the same. The ticket to the technology is change.

When we transform, we can hear the same exact thing we heard a month, a year, a decade ago, but it will sound different, and resonate deeper. But when we get stuck in ruts, patterns, and complacency, our learning stays stuck as well. What is the difference between humans and animals? Animals do the same thing day after day after day. But we have a choice.

Today, shake up your routines. If you always start the day with coffee, then start with tea. If you always read the newspaper, skip it. If you flop in front of the TV when you get home, then open a book, or better yet, go for a walk. Get in the habit of mixing it up and changing yourself. The wisdom will change accordingly.

When I was a child, I would sometimes awaken in the middle of the night, horrified by the fear that I'd find someone in my room. I'd pull the covers over my head and shake in terror. When nothing happened, I'd peek out and see some clothing draped over a chair or some other object masquerading as a monster.

Focusing the Light of awareness on that which frightens us dissolves the misunderstanding that causes it.

What monster do you need to stare down?

Imagine an old lady on the corner of a busy intersection. A passerby attempts to help her cross the street safely. She politely refuses. He tries again. She still refuses, now somewhat annoyed at his insistence.

Why is she annoyed? Because she has no desire to cross the street. She's merely standing at the intersection, waiting for the bus to arrive.

Sometimes, in our zeal to share, we end up forcing our kindness on people who don't want it. For real sharing to take place, there must be a willing receiver, and an actual desire to take possession of the offering.

Pay attention to how you give today. Make sure there's someone receiving on the other end.

Why is it so hard to say "I love you?" I don't mean to a lover, but to a friend, a teacher, a parent. Why are these four little letters so difficult to spit out of our mouths?

What a wonderful gift to give someone. Think about how good it feels when people say it to you. I love you. Sometimes, when you have strife with family, or a beef with a friend, saying "I love you" is all you need to do to take away the darkness that has settled in like a fog. We fight and argue and analyze when, usually, "I love you" will do the trick.

Who do you love and cherish, yet are afraid to tell how you feel? Take a risk today. Open your heart, open your mouth, and say it. Just say it. I LOVE YOU!

More Books That Can Help You Bring the Wisdom of Kabbalah into your Life

Living Kabbalah: A Practical System for Making the Power Work for You
By Yehuda Berg

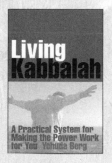

Living Kabbalah is a unique system of technology meant for you to use to transform your life and achieve true and lasting fulfillment. In these pages, you will find practical tools and exercises to help you break negative patterns, overcome challenges, and incorporate the time-tested wisdom of Kabbalah into your daily life. Noted author and teacher Yehuda Berg provides a clear blueprint that guides you step-by-step along the path toward the ultimate attainment of all that you need and desire.

Tap into a greater power—the power of Kabbalah—and learn to live more fully, richly, and joyfully every day, starting today!

The Living Kabbalah System™: Levels 1, 2 & 3

Take Your Life to the Next Level™ with this step-by-step, 23-day system for transforming your life and achieving lasting fulfillment.

Created by Yehuda Berg and based on his belief that Kabbalah should be lived, not merely studied, this revolutionary interactive system incorporates the latest learning strategies, addressing all three learning styles:

- Auditory (recorded audio sessions)

- Visual (workbook with written concepts and graphics)

- Tactile (written exercises, self-assessments, and physical tools)

The sturdy carrying case makes the system easy and convenient to use, in the car, at the gym, on a plane, wherever and whenever you choose. Learn from today's great Kabbalah leaders in an intimate, one-on-one learning atmosphere. You get practical, actionable tools and exercises to integrate the wisdom of Kabbalah into your daily life. In just 23 days you can learn to live with greater intensity, be more successful in business and relationships, and achieve your dreams. Why wait? Take your life to the next level starting today.

Days of Connection
By Michael Berg

The ancient wisdom of Kabbalah teaches that each month of the lunar year holds different opportunities for us to grow and change and, conversely, holds unique pitfalls for getting stalled on our journey toward spiritual transformation. The special power of each month is strongest at its beginning, the time of the new moon, known as Rosh Chodesh. And holidays are unmatched as windows in time that make specific kinds of spiritual energy available to us. In *Days of Connection*, Michael Berg guides us through the kabbalistic calendar and explains the meaning and power behind all of these special days.

Nano: Technology of Mind over Matter
By Rav Berg

Kabbalah is all about attaining control over the physical world, including our personal lives, at the most fundamental level of reality. It's about achieving and extending mind over matter and developing the ability to create fulfillment, joy, and happiness by controlling everything at the most basic level of existence. In this way, Kabbalah predates and presages the most exciting trend in recent scientific and technological development, the application of nanotechnology to all areas of life in order to create better, stronger, and more efficient results.

Simple Light
By Karen Berg

From the woman regarded by many as their "spiritual mother," and whose work has touched millions of lives around the world, here is a book with a message that is simple and straight from the heart: It's all about love and sharing.

Karen's unique voice will serve to inspire you and help you to face life's daily challenges. Open the book to any passage whenever you find a moment, and you will begin to discover the keys to leading a more joyful and fulfilled life.

The Power of Kabbalah
By Yehuda Berg

Imagine your life filled with unending joy, purpose, and contentment. Imagine your days infused with pure insight and energy. This is *The Power of Kabbalah*. It is the path from the momentary pleasure that most of us settle for, to the lasting fulfillment that is yours to claim. Your deepest desires are waiting to be realized. Find out how, in this basic introduction to the ancient wisdom of Kabbalah.

Rebooting: Defeating Depression with the Power of Kabbalah
By Yehuda Berg

An estimated 18 million people in the United States suffer from depression—that's almost 10% of the population. So chances are good that you have, or someone you know has, been affected by it. Antidepressants, counseling, herbal remedies—all have been known to help treat the symptoms, but sometimes they fall short. If only you could click on the "Restart" button and get your internal software back on track. Now, in *Rebooting*, noted kabbalistic scholar and author Yehuda Berg shows how you can do just that by reconnecting with desire and light to emerge from this debilitating darkness.

The Secret: Unlocking the Source of Joy & Fulfillment
By Michael Berg

The Secret reveals the essence of life in its most concise and powerful form. Several years before the latest "Secret" phenomenon, Michael Berg shared the amazing truths of the world's oldest spiritual wisdom in this book. In it, he has pieced together an ancient puzzle to show that our common understanding of life's purpose is actually backwards, and that anything less than complete joy and fulfillment can be changed by correcting this misperception.

The Zohar

Composed more than 2,000 years ago, the *Zohar* is a set of 23 books, a commentary on biblical and spiritual matters in the form of conversations among spiritual masters. But to describe the *Zohar* only in physical terms is greatly misleading. In truth, the *Zohar* is nothing less than a powerful tool for achieving the most important purposes of our lives. It was given to all humankind by the Creator to bring us protection, to connect us with the Creator's Light, and ultimately to fulfill our birthright of true spiritual transformation.

More than eighty years ago, when The Kabbalah Centre was founded, the *Zohar* had virtually disappeared from the world. Few people in the general population had ever heard of it. Whoever sought to read it—in any country, in any language, at any price—faced a long and futile search.

Today all this has changed. Through the work of The Kabbalah Centre and the editorial efforts of Michael Berg, the *Zohar* is now being brought to the world, not only in the original Aramaic language but also in English. The new English *Zohar* provides everything for connecting to this sacred text on all levels: the original Aramaic text for scanning; an English translation; and clear, concise commentary for study and learning.

The Kabbalah Centre®

The Kabbalah Centre® is a spiritual organization dedicated to bringing the wisdom of Kabbalah to the world. The Kabbalah Centre® itself has existed for more than 80 years, but its spiritual lineage extends back to Rav Isaac Luria in the 16th century and even further back to Rav Shimon bar Yochai, who revealed the principal text of Kabbalah, the *Zohar*, more than 2,000 years ago.

The Kabbalah Centre® was founded in 1922 by Rav Yehuda Ashlag, one of the greatest kabbalists of the 20th Century. When Rav Ashlag left this world, leadership of The Kabbalah Centre® was taken on by Rav Yehuda Brandwein. Before his passing, Rav Brandwein designated Rav Berg as director of The Kabbalah Centre®. Now, for more than 30 years, The Kabbalah Centre® has been under the direction of Rav Berg, his wife Karen Berg, and their sons, Yehuda Berg and Michael Berg.

Although there are many scholarly studies of Kabbalah, The Kabbalah Centre® does not teach Kabbalah as an academic discipline but as a way of creating a better life. The mission of The Kabbalah Centre® is to make the practical tools and spiritual teachings of Kabbalah available and accessible to everyone regardless of religion, ethnicity, gender or age.

The Kabbalah Centre® makes no promises. But if people are willing to work hard to grow and become actively sharing, caring and tolerant human beings, Kabbalah teaches that they will then experience fulfillment and joy in a way previously unknown to them. This sense of fulfillment, however, comes gradually and is always the result of the student's spiritual work.

Our ultimate goal is for all humanity to gain the happiness and fulfillment that is our true destiny.

Kabbalah teaches its students to question and test everything they learn. One of the most important teachings of Kabbalah is that there is no coercion in spirituality.

What Does The Kabbalah Centre® Offer?

Local Kabbalah Centres around the world offer onsite lectures, classes, study groups, holiday celebrations and services, and a community of teachers and fellow students. To find a Centre near you, go to www.kabbalah.com.

For those of you unable to access a physical Kabbalah Centre due to the constraints of location or time, we have other ways to participate in The Kabbalah Centre® community.

At www.kabbalah.com, we feature online blogs, newsletters, weekly wisdom, a store, and much more.

It's a wonderful way to stay tuned in and in touch, and it gives you access to programs that will expand your mind and challenge you to continue your spiritual work.

Student Support

The Kabbalah Centre® empowers people to take responsibility for their own lives. It's about the teachings, not the teachers. But on your journey to personal growth, things can be unclear and sometimes rocky, so it is helpful to have a coach or teacher. Simply call 1 800 KABBALAH toll free.

All Student Support instructors have studied Kabbalah under the direct supervision of Kabbalist Rav Berg, widely recognized as the preeminent kabbalist of our time.

We have also created opportunities for you to interact with other Student Support students through study groups, monthly connections, holiday retreats, and other events held around the country.